COLLINS PO...

LETTER WRITING

Louise Bostock Lang

HarperCollins*Publishers*

HarperCollins Publishers
P.O. Box, Glasgow G4 0NB

First published 1994

Reprint 10 9 8 7 6 5 4 3

© HarperCollins Publishers 1994

ISBN 0 00 470702 8

A catalogue record for this book is available
from the British Library

Printed in Hong Kong

CONTENTS

Introduction 5

Letter-Writing Techniques
Materials and Implements 8
Layout and Component Parts 26
Planning a Communication 41
Punctuation and Spelling 50
Grammar and Style 73
Addressing an Envelope 91
Notes for Office Workers 109
Writing Letters Abroad 138
The Law on Letter Writing 150

Letters for all Occasions
Accepting a Position 159
Acknowledgments 160
Apologies 163
Appeals and Fundraising 166
Associations and Societies 169
Bon Voyage 176
Bookings 178
Change of Address 182
Classified Advertisements 184
Complaints 190
Condolence 193
Congratulations 196
Cover notes 200
Disputes 201
Divorce 203
Filling in Forms 204
Form Letters 206

3

CONTENTS

Get-Well Letters 207
Good Luck 210
Information 211
Insurance 216
Invitations 219
Job Applications 226
Legal Letters 248
Letters Home 250
Love Letters 252
Memoranda 253
Neighbours 255
Newspaper Announcements 257
Postcards 260
Press Releases 261
Quotations and Estimates 267
Redundancy and Dismissal 269
References and Testimonials 272
Remittance Advice 280
Reprimands 281
Resignations 284
Thank-you Letters 286
To a Pen Pal 291
To Authorities 294
To a Young Child 295
To MPs 296
To Royalty 298
To the Bank 299
To the Press 303
To Utility Companies 305
To your Child's School 307
Wedding Correspondence 309

INTRODUCTION

The writing of letters is a human activity that dates back thousands of years – probably as far back as the introduction of writing as a form of communication. Nowadays millions of people write and despatch letters every day, bound for an equal number of destinations all over the world – business letters, political letters, love letters, invitations, thanks, news. The international postal service is so efficient that a letter travels half-way around the world from Sydney, Australia to London, UK in just five days. And if a facsimile transmission is the mode of communication, a letter can arrive within seconds of its being sent.

There are several competing forms of communication in the modern world – telephone, telex, computer mailbox – but there is nothing quite like an old-fashioned letter to get the message, whatever it might be, across.

There are two main reasons why this may be the case. First, there is a romance surrounding writing and receiving letters that a message left on a computer noticeboard simply does not have; people who correspond may even be said to be contributing to a literary tradition that has been in the making for centuries.

Second, letters are capable of transmitting not only a written message, but also a whole host of other, peripheral, messages about the writer and his or her attitude towards the recipient. From the colour and quality of the stationery to the style of the signature and the efficiency of delivery, every letter has a 'hidden story' to tell.

Collins Pocket Reference Letter Writing covers both business and personal letters. It gives advice on how to compose a good letter for many occasions and circumstances. The first half of the book – **Letter-Writing Techniques** – covers general techniques that will make the reader a skilled and efficient letter-writer. It covers planning and laying out a letter, choosing an appropriate form of address, common errors in written English and how to make your written style effective. It also gives advice on writing letters to send abroad and outlines the law as it relates to written correspondence .

The second half of the book is an A–Z of possible occasions on which you might like to write a letter. Each entry gives ideas on what to say and points out any pitfalls that you may come across. Where possible, sample letters are given, for adaptation to particular circumstances. The sample letters act as a guide to what to say – the substance of the letter. For details of where to correctly place addresses, dates, reference numbers and closing elements, see the layouts on pp. 38-40 in **Letter-Writing Techniques.** Letters that should be typed appear in a plain typeface, although there is no hard-and-fast rule against handwriting some of these formal types of letter. Letters that are better handwritten appear in a scripted type-face.

All elements of the book are cross-referenced so that the reader can hop from general information in **Letter-Writing Techniques** to specific advice in **Letters for all Occasions.**

LETTER-WRITING TECHNIQUES

MATERIALS AND IMPLEMENTS

Today's market in greetings cards offers a spectacular range of products. There are cards for numerous occasions: birthdays, retirements, bereavements, passing exams, good luck cards, even cards that say in the most poetic fashion everything you would like to say to a loved-one but don't know how. There are so many greetings and message cards on the market, in fact, that it would seem that the personal letter-writer has no need to compose a single letter on any occasion – let the manufacturers do it all for you.

However tempting this may at first appear, there are many occasions, even personal or informal ones, on which it is not appropriate simply to throw a signed card in the post. This chapter deals with the many other forms of stationery available for both personal and business use, and suggests some of the things to think about when looking around for suitable supplies.

The golden rule

In all correspondence, there is one golden rule: remember the recipient. When choosing stationery supplies or styles of letterhead for business correspondence, always consider first and foremost the people to whom you will be writing. Letters have a 'body-language' all of their own: lavender-coloured paper with a faint hint of scent, for instance, transmits a totally different message to white A4 with a no-nonsense letterhead, and this message will be received loud and clear even before the addressee begins to read. Business stationery will be dealt with in the second part of this chapter. First, here are some tips for personal letter-writers.

Writing paper and envelopes

Personal stationery is generally smaller than business stationery, and there is a choice of colours. Unless it is really the image you want to project, avoid bright or particularly 'romantic' colours; these will only distract your reader's attention from what you are saying, and are certainly not appropriate for those letters of complaint to your MP or a utility company. A good basic writing-paper is white, cream or blue. As a rule, go for the best quality stationery you can afford; a watermark is always a good sign. Recycled paper is ideal for more informal letters.

Make sure that whatever colour you use, you have envelopes that match not only in colour, but also in paper quality and size. Each manufacturer has a different method of categorizing writing-paper sizes. Some use small-standard-large, while others may use 1-2-3. The packaging of the envelopes that match the paper should give the corresponding size category.

Your choice of size depends once again on the kinds of letters you will be writing. If your letters tend to be short, choose one of the smaller sizes, as a short two-paragraph message will look lost on paper approaching A4. Equally, if you tend to write a lot of more formal letters, you may wish to invest in a larger size to avoid the need to cram everything into a small space or to use several sheets. In this case, it is a good idea to invest in personalized A4 stationery. This means that your letters are the same size as most other business letters and so are less likely to get lost, are easier to file, and are generally taken more seriously than letters on smaller paper.

Avoid lined paper, which suggests you cannot write in a straight line without help, and tends to remind people of junior school handwriting classes. Most pads of writing-paper come with a sheet that is ruled, and if you do find your lines tend to droop, slip this sheet under the page you are writing on to act as a guide.

Cards and postcards

The letter writer is not confined to writing paper and envelopes, however. It is a good idea to keep a small number of plain white postcards or the beautiful postcards now produced by art galleries and museums, for replying to invitations or for very short messages.

Notelets are folded into four, so that the image shows on the front, and the writer has four times the space to write on when they are opened out. They are most often sold in packages of five or ten with matching envelopes, and can be very attractive.

If you tend to entertain people regularly in your own home, a stock of printed 'At Home' cards, would come in handy. These can be bought ready-printed with only the details (who, where and when) to fill in, or they can be ordered from a printer for a special occasion. (See **Invitations** pp 220-21.)

For those who are not only fond of writing letters or sending cards, but are also embroidery enthusiasts, it is now possible to buy plain cards with a window in which to mount small embroidered pieces. These make beautiful greetings cards to be framed and treasured. They are available from craft suppliers.

In the same vein, painters can now obtain from art suppliers and mail-order catalogues plain cards to decorate themselves.

Paper for letters overseas

If you find yourself frequently writing abroad, airmail paper saves money on postage (which is paid according to weight). It is normally found in blue or sometimes white, and comes in a variety of sizes. Airmail envelopes are also lightweight, and should have the words Airmail/Par Avion, printed in the top left-hand corner. If you are using ordinary envelopes for international mail, remember to obtain a sticker bearing these words and attach it to the envelope in this position.

An alternative to airmail paper is the aerogramme, a single sheet of lightweight paper that folds up to become its own envelope. Aerogrammes were first introduced in the UK during World War II to encourage those at home to write to people stationed abroad. Aerogrammes can be bought from stationers, but those purchased at the Post Office have the postage already paid at a special single rate for every country in the world, so there is no need to buy stamps. On top of this, it is possible to buy packages of six aerogrammes, which are sold at an even cheaper rate than single aerogrammes.

For those who write to people overseas with the Armed Forces, the Post Office supplies special envelopes. It is not necessary to pay postage on letters sent in such envelopes, but you must use a particular station address to qualify for free postage, and there are weight restrictions.

See also **Writing Letters Abroad**, **To a Pen Pal**, **Letters Home**.

Personalized stationery

Stationery that has been printed with your address and telephone number saves you time, avoids confusion that may arise through semi-legible handwriting, and also gives a good impression. If you don't own a typewriter or word-processor and are therefore forced to write even formal correspondence by hand, personalized stationery adds a touch of formality to your letters. So if you do find yourself writing formal letters but in a personal capacity, having your stationery personalized is very worthwhile.

Most printers and print-bureaux will print a box of paper, and are able to show the customer a wide range of print styles (fonts) and layouts. They will also advise on weight and colour of paper and appropriate matching envelopes. However, shop around before making up your mind which printer to use. Prices vary enormously from company to company and you may find a jobbing printer cheaper than a High Street bureau, especially if you can wait a couple of weeks.

BUYING PERSONALIZED STATIONERY

When buying personalized stationery, it is always a good idea to purchase a quantity of paper that matches your personalized paper, but with no printing on it. This is for use when you want to add a second or third sheet to a letter – the convention is that such continuation sheets do not give your address.

There are three techniques available for printing stationery: printing, engraving and a new technique that closely resembles engraving, but is much cheaper. The first technique is standard, and differs from engraving in that when letters are engraved they stand out from the surface of the paper. Engraving is widely considered to be of better quality than printing and is probably a good choice for wedding stationery (see **Wedding Correspondence** pp. 312-14), but most people find it too expensive for everyday use.

There is a choice of position and layout for your address. It may be placed centred at the head of the sheet, or 'ranged right' in the right-hand corner. Avoid having your address printed on the left-hand side of the paper, because in formal letters this is the usual place to write the addressee's details (see pp. 30-31). Some people also have a quantity of blank postcards personalized with their address. In this case, the address should be positioned along the top edge of the card, in one line if possible.

When choosing a font and the colour of the printing, follow the golden rule and consider the recipient. A frothy font full of scrolls and flourishes might look pretty, but it might also be difficult to read (your recipient may not have English as his or her first language), and will perhaps convey your personality as frivolous or even pompous. There are many less affected fonts that can lend your stationery style and grace, without going to extremes of whimsy. By the same token, it is possible to have your stationery personalized in a variety of colours. The first consideration when choosing colours may be one of cost: black alone is always the cheapest, and a combination of two or more colours is inevitably the most expensive. Second, if you are determined to choose a colour, make sure that it does not clash violently with the colour of the paper, and that it will be palatable to your recipients.

KEY POINTS: CHOOSING STATIONERY AND PRINTING

- Consider the kinds of letter you most often write and buy stationery that suits the purpose.

- Match the size of the envelope to the size of the paper.

- Keep a stock of cards and notelets for short messages sent on impulse.

- Aerogrammes are cheaper than airmail letters, especially if bought in packs of six.

- Remember the recipient and consider the impression your stationery will leave behind.

Business stationery

It is fair to say that no business is taken seriously unless its correspondence is typed on formal printed stationery. The extent of a company's business stationery depends on the company's size and age. You may be a self-employed painter and decorator working from home, and in this case a letterhead may well be all you will need. However, an established company will probably have a wide range of stationery items printed. *What*

exactly is printed on company stationery is a matter of convention, and *how* it is printed is a matter of corporate identity.

This section describes the most common items of company
stationery, what should be printed on each one, and how this
is best done.

Designing company stationery

If you are setting up a new company or wish to revamp your
company's existing letterhead, it is a good idea to consult a
team of designers or a typographer. You will need to discuss
with the person you choose the nature of your business and
the image you wish to put across to your public. (If you are in
the process of reworking your company's entire marketing
image, the style of the stationery will be an integral part of
those changes.) From such discussions an experienced designer should be able to come up with a number of typographical
'solutions' from which to choose.

The designer may also be able to offer you printing services
as part of the package, or you may decide to contract your own
printer to do the work. There are a number of options here: a
jobbing printer, who may be relatively slow, but on the whole
cheaper than a High Street bureau; a bureau, which will be
able to offer speed at a price; or a stationery supplier.

With the advent of desk-top publishing, it is also now
possible to print your own stationery, but on the whole, you
will probably find that the cost of laser printing large quantities is higher than using traditional methods, and unless you
have the use of a very high-quality printer, you will probably
not achieve such professional results.

Many companies make use of a logo, that is, a design or
image that illustrates the business or refers to the company's
'identity' in some way. Creating logos is an art-form in its own
right, and designers, artists and marketing and advertising
companies can command large fees for producing one. If you

are considering a logo for your stationery, always consult someone who has a track record in this type of work.

When making your final decision on style do not overlook the basic fact that the wording on stationery is for the recipient's information, and so must be easily legible and laid out in a logical order.

Using colour

If you are tempted to choose colour printing for your letterhead, remember that colour is much more expensive than black, and that you will bear this extra cost each time you order more stationery. Remember also to choose appropriate colours, and ones that are acceptable to the vast majority of people.

Choosing paper

After typography, logo and colour, the next most important item to consider is the quality of the paper you wish your company to use for letters. There are many types of paper on the market, and each of these is usually specified by weight in grams per square metre (gsm). The weight of paper usually used for letters ranges from 70 to 110 gsm – the heavier the paper, the better-quality it appears to be. Lighter papers are available, but are generally not used for correspondence: 'bank' paper (40–45 gsm) is used for carbon copies or file copies; duplicating paper (60–70 gsm) is used for photocopies; and the lightest paper generally available (25–30 gsm) is used for airmail letters.

Letterheads and continuation sheets

These are the items of stationery that staff will probably use most. A letterhead is generally A4 sized, and is normally used for ordinary letters and faxes. However, some companies also send out short letters such as acknowledgements (see pp. 160-

62) and remittance advice (see p. 280) on A5 (half the size of A4) or on 2/3A4.

The letterhead should contain the following information:

- The company's name and full postal address (if the main entrance is difficult to find, a short explanation could be given: '19 Commercial Road, entrance on Howard Street', for instance).
- Telephone number(s), fax number(s) and telex number(s) as appropriate.
- The company's registered address (if different) and registration number.
- If the business is a sole trader, then there may be a description of the business: 'E. A. Flint & Company, Painters & Decorators', for example.
- If the business is a partnership, the letterhead may give the names of the senior partners, and, if it is a charity, the patron's name may be added.

Continuation sheets are used when more than one sheet is not enough (although many adhere to the rule that if you can't say what you need to say on one page, you are using too many words). Continuation sheets may be either blank sheets of the same paper as is used for the letterhead, or sheets printed with just the name of the company or its logo.

There are various options when it comes to deciding where to place the information required on a letterhead: at the head of the page and centred; at the head of the page at the right-hand side; or at the foot of the page. Some designers choose to split letterhead information, perhaps placing the company name and logo at the head of the page, and giving the other information at the foot. The one rule is to avoid placing the information at the top left-hand side, because this space is reserved for the addressee's details (sometimes known as the 'inside address').

When these considerations have been ironed out with regard to the standard letterhead, it is normal to follow the same style and positioning for all other items of stationery.

Compliments slips

Compliments slips are used to accompany printed information or other enclosures that require little explanation. They are usually printed on A7 (74 x 105 mm), and normally only give the company's contact information and the words 'With Compliments'. It is not necessary to write on compliments slips, but a signature with the date is sometimes helpful.

Envelopes

A printed envelope is a sign that a company is truly established and prospering. The company name and address should be positioned in the top left-hand corner on the front of the envelope or across the top of the flap on the back. These conventions should not be broken, because other areas of the envelope are reserved for postage and the recipient's address. It is not necessary to give telephone or other information on envelopes.

If you are not keen to go to the expense of printing envelopes, an alternative method of helping the postal service in the event that letters are returned is to have stickers or parcel labels produced that give return information.

If you find yourself ordering envelopes for an office that produces a large number of form letters, staff may thank you for supplying them with 'window' envelopes. When the inside address is typed in the correct position on the letter, and it is folded correctly, the address shows through the envelope's transparent window, and this will obviate the need to type out separate envelopes. You might also think about helping staff further by supplying a special letterhead that has a box drawn to show the position of the 'window'.

PAPER AND ENVELOPE SIZES

Most paper and envelopes are now sized according to the European metric system. Paper sizes begin with the letter A, and A0 is the largest. Each subsequent size (A1, A2, A3, etc.) is half the size of the previous one. The one exception to the rule is the new size, 2/3A4, sometimes used by banks for bank statements.

Envelope sizes are prefixed with the letter C. It is the convention when specifying envelope sizes in millimetres to give the side with the flap as the second measurement. Envelopes in sizes C6 and C5/6 are the formats preferred by the Royal Mail.

The following table gives sizes of envelopes and the sizes of paper that can be used with them.

Envelope	Size (mm)	Paper	Size (mm)	Folds
C3	324 x 458 mm	A3	297 x 420 mm	unfolded
C4	229 x 324 mm	A4	210 x 297 mm	unfolded
C5	162 x 229 mm	A4	210 x 297 mm	1 fold
		A5	148 x 210 mm	unfolded
C6	114 x 162 mm	A4	210 x 297 mm	2 folds
		A5	148 x 210 mm	1 fold
		A6	105 x 148 mm	unfolded
C5/6	110 x 220 mm	A7	74 x 105 mm	unfolded
		2/3A4	210 x 198 mm	1 fold
		A5	148 x 210 mm	1 fold
		A4	210 x 297 mm	2 folds (into thirds)

Facsimile front sheets

Many companies use the letter layout for facsimiles, and some print 'front sheets' as part of their stationery. Front sheets give information about the transmission, including: sender's name and extension number; addressee's name, fax number, company name and sometimes address; contact number for the sender for use if the transmission is not successful.

Writing implements

Not so long ago, anyone wishing to hand-write anything had only two alternatives, a fountain pen or a pencil. Now, however, a wide range of writing implements is available to choose from, and many are relatively cheap. Most people these days pick up the nearest biro to write or sign a letter, but there is a lot to be said for selecting a pen that you enjoy handling and that enhances your handwriting. It goes without saying that a person with legible handwriting is considered more effective and efficient (and more likely to have that crucial job application succeed, for example), and that somebody with a no-nonsense signature is a no-nonsense kind of person, to be treated accordingly.

First of all, never use a pencil when writing letters, however informal. Writing in ink has always been considered an essential courtesy, and even in these less formal days, a letter in pencil would receive scant attention. Biros should also be avoided, especially if your handwriting leaves something to be desired. They will not improve legibility, and they tend to give a bland and rather ugly line. However, there are a number of modern ballpoint pens with a range of tip sizes that can produce an attractive line and are hardwearing into the bargain.

Tip sizes are usually given in tenths of a millimetre: 0.3 mm is a good size for general use. A tip of just 0.1 mm is probably too small for letter-writing, and should be reserved for technical purposes. Choose a pen with a tip that is guaranteed not to spread – it is annoying when a person's handwriting increases in size in the course of a letter to accommodate a tip that has become wider.

Next in the scale comes a new range of 'fountain pens' with a plastic tip that gives a broad or fine line. These are useful if your handwriting looks better with a broad line and they imitate the style of a fountain pen extremely well.

One of the obvious advantages of these types of pen is that they do not need to be filled with ink, and they don't blot on the paper. However, some use ink that may 'bleed' (spread out) on some kinds of paper. Another drawback is that the ink may show through onto the other side of the paper. Most people do not write on both sides of the paper, but if you do, this could be a consideration. If you are looking around, therefore, take a small piece of your favourite writing paper with you and test any pen you are thinking about buying.

Fountain pens

The old-fashioned fountain pen is still a good choice for letter-writers (even if all your letters are typed and all you do is sign them). A good-quality fountain pen should last a lifetime. The market has broadened considerably in the last decade or so, and it is now also possible to buy 'chunky' fountain pens which are easier to hold. These might be a good choice for children or for older people who may have difficulty gripping the more slender models.

It is possible to buy nibs in a variety of widths, and the one you choose depends on your style of handwriting. Once again, it is a good idea to test a fountain pen before you buy it, and after you have chosen it, do not let others use it. Just as a pair of shoes gives to accommodate the shape of the wearer's feet and his or her gait, a high-quality nib will change shape slightly to accommodate the unique way in which you write. If another person uses your pen, you may find that it has moulded itself in a different way, making your handwriting look awkward.

Calligraphy pens

For those who are really interested in working on their handwriting, a range of calligraphy pens is available from art suppliers, with long barrels for a firm grip and a selection of nibs including an italic nib which gives a sharp distinction between different angles of stroke. However, don't go too far into the realms of art. While calligraphy pens can help you to improve your handwriting, they may also encourage you to add frivolous flourishes that are not appropriate in many contexts.

Coloured inks

The wide range of colours available for fountain pens, calligraphy pens, biros and ballpoints is taken for granted these days. However, it is still unusual for letter-writers to use any colour except black or blue. If there is a distinction to be drawn between colours used for informal and formal letter-writing, it is that formal letters should be written in black ink, while it is acceptable to use blue for informal letters. Other colours should really only be used in an informal context, and then with great care: red or green ink would be less appropriate for a letter of condolence (see pp. 193-5) than for a letter to a pen pal (see pp. 291-3), for example.

Good handwriting

However widespread the use of typewriters and word processors becomes, it will be a very long time indeed before handwriting becomes a thing of the past. Even if you type the most personal of your correspondence, you still need to pick up a pen to sign it, and there is always that job advertisement that specifies the handwritten covering letter.

Many people are reluctant to write letters because they feel their handwriting is not up to scratch. However, if you follow a few rules, you will probably find that your handwriting improves:

- Write slowly and try to keep the letters all the same size.
- Make a quick rough draft of your letter first (you will be tempted to write faster as the ideas come up), and then take your time over the 'fair copy'.
- Don't write so big that you can only get three or four words to a line, but don't write so small that a magnifying glass is needed to read it. However, when writing to children or to people with vision impairment, you may need to write bigger than you usually do.
- The lines that rise above and drop below the line should not interfere with the lines of writing above and below.
- Make sure that the spaces between the words are a constant size.
- Try to keep a reasonably constant distance between each line of your letter.
- Avoid crossing out or altering wrong letters – this is unsightly.
- Keep your signature legible, and avoid flourishes – it should not be very different from the rest of your hand writing. Practice your signature, and once you are happy with it, stick to it.
- Choose a good pen that improves your handwriting, rather than picking up the nearest ballpoint, which can only make your writing worse.

Typewriters and word processors

All business letters should be typed, and formal letters in a personal context (to the bank manager, your child's school, to your doctor or local authority, for example) receive more attention if produced with a typewriter or word processor.

There has been a huge increase in the numbers of type writers and word processors available. Luckily for the personal letter writer, many machines have also become so cheap that most households can afford one. Here are some things to look for when buying a typing machine:

- Typeface or variety of typefaces available. Find a machine that gives you a clear and stylish typeface, or a selection to choose from.
- Correction facilities. All word processors enable you to correct your work at any stage before (or after) printing, and many electric and electronic typewriters have a facility that enables you to correct your writing line by line.
- Availability of foreign characters. If you write to people abroad, you may need to use foreign accents (e.g. é, â, ç, etc.). Many people make do with writing them in by hand, but your letters will look better if you find a word processor that can generate such characters (normally using the 'alternative keyboard'), or buy a golfball typewriter that enables you to change the ball when necessary.
- Printer standard. There is a wide range of printers available (daisywheel, golfball, bubblejet, laser), and they vary a great deal in price. Think carefully about the quality of printing you require, and as a rule, buy the best you can afford.
- Memory. Electronic typewriters are so sophisticated these days that for the letter-writer it is almost unnecessary to invest in a word processor. However, the main difference between the two – the ability of the word processor to 'remember' and 'file' all the documents you have saved to the memory – may be of importance if you write a large number of very similar letters or need a number of copies of each letter you write. A word processor will also save you time normally used for letters: while it is

still important to work out the main points you want to raise before you start typing, you can revise your letter as you go along.

- Portability. Consider where and when you will be using the machine, and where you will store it. You may travel a great deal, and so a portable battery-operated machine might serve a useful purpose. Alternatively, you may not have space at home to keep a machine permanently on your desk or kitchen table, so you will need a small, light machine that you can store away when not in use.

- Word-processing software. The second main difference between typewriters and word processors is that you will have to learn to use the word-processing software (the commands that ask the machine to do what you want.) These days software is extremely user-friendly, and most people can learn to use it in a very short time. However, if this is the first time you have used a computer, discuss software packages with the supplier – he or she may be able to recommend a suitable package.

When to write, when to type

Deciding on whether to write or to type your letter is mostly a matter of convention. As a general rule, business and formal letters should always be typed. Informal letters should be handwritten, but in some circumstances typing a personal letter is acceptable, especially if your handwriting is tortuous. There are one or two instances, however, when a letter *must* be handwritten (a letter of condolence on a bereavement, for example). The second part of this book looks at a great many different kinds of letter, and gives the conventions on whether to handwrite or type.

Collecting materials and implements for writing letters is a matter of deciding what is acceptable or suitable for the kinds of letters you are going to write. Some thought in this direction will mean that you are likely to have the right materials to hand when you want to write (and therefore no excuses for not writing), and that your letters are more likely to be enjoyable to read or to receive the attention they deserve.

LAYOUT AND COMPONENT PARTS

Every letter is made up of a number of components, and there are rules that govern where, how and why these components are used. Such rules are actually conventions, observed to ensure that information is conveyed rapidly and effectively. Breaking the rules is sometimes acceptable, but in formal and business correspondence, it is probably wise not to do so without a good reason.

This chapter deals with how to lay out a letter, whether it is handwritten or typed. Exceptions to these rules are invitations, CVs, press releases and some other forms of correspondence. The A–Z in the second half of this book gives details of special layouts where necessary. Later in this chapter, each of the component parts of a letter is described, along with guidelines for their use. Understanding what these are enables letters to be written with greater ease and digested more quickly by the recipient.

Layout

There are two styles of layout now in common use: the fully-blocked layout and the semi-blocked layout. Informal handwritten letters are best laid out in the semi-blocked style. When typing a letter, it is possible to choose between the two layouts, but if you are writing letters on behalf of a company, check back in the filing to find out which the company prefers to use. If you need to send a formal letter but cannot get to a typing machine (or, perhaps, if a prospective employer asks you to handwrite a covering letter to a CV [see pp. 240-43]), it is best to use the fully-blocked style.

Semi-blocked layout

In this format, each paragraph is indented from the left-hand edge of the page. The subscription (yours sincerely, yours faithfully, etc. [see pp. 34-5]) and the signatory (the typed version of the sender's name placed after the signature are also indented. The date and any reference number is placed on the same line at the top of the page and the subject heading is centred under the salutation. (The sample letter on p. 38 is laid out in semi-blocked style, and is followed by a handwritten letter in this format.)

When using the semi-blocked style, it is usual to punctuate using 'standard punctuation' (see below).

Fully-blocked layout

This format is now more widely used in the business context because it tends to look less informal. Each paragraph of this style of letter is started flush left rather than indented. A line space is left between each paragraph. The subscription, signatory and subject heading are also typed flush left, and the reference and date have a line to themselves. (The sample letter on p. 39 is laid out in fully-blocked style, the letter on p. 40 shows a letter on headed paper in this format.)

If your letter is typed using the fully-blocked layout, it is usual to use 'open punctuation' (see below).

Punctuation of addresses and other details

There are two styles of punctuation in common use. The first, 'standard punctuation' is usually used for letters that are laid out in the semi-blocked style (see above). It consists of adding commas to the ends of the lines of an address, after the salutation and subscription, and in the date. The second style, known as 'open punctuation', entails no punctuation at all (this style is preferred by the Royal Mail when addressing envelopes). (The sample letters on pp. 38 and 39-40 are punctuated using standard and open punctuation respectively.)

MARGINS

It is normal to leave a good margin on either side of the wording of your letter. This is especially important with business correspondence when space must be left for the recipient to punch holes in the left-hand side for filing, and may be needed on the right-hand side for the recipient's own notes. Also, pay attention to the margins at the top and bottom of the sheet. As a general rule, leave more space at the foot of the paper than at the head. Balancing the size of the margins is just a matter of trial and error until you find a formula that looks good with the size and shape of the paper you are using.

Component parts

Each letter written will make use of one or more of the following components. Some of the notes that follow relate merely to position, while others give details of conventions regarding forms of words. Those composing business letters will use most of these components, whereas an informal or personal letter may omit some of the details.

Sender's address

This is the first item written in a letter. Handwritten letters normally give the address in the top right-hand corner. It is normal to indent each successive line of the address by about three characters. Remember to start a good distance in from the right-hand margin so that the last line of the address, which starts closest to the right-hand side, is not cramped. (See p. 38 for information on how best to write out an address.)

Personalized stationery or company letterhead give the sender's address already printed. (See pp. 15-16 for the information the letterhead should contain.)

> ### TELEPHONE NUMBERS
> It is usual to omit your telephone number from your address on a handwritten letter. However, if you use personalized stationery, you may add your telephone number on a line after the postcode. The dialling code can be given in brackets or separated from the rest of the number by a space or dash. It is not necessary to use the word 'Tel.' or 'Telephone' before giving the number, but some people use a small telephone icon, and this can be effective with certain styles of printing.

Letter reference

The first reference number normally found on a business letter is that of the sender's office. Many businesses make use of a reference to indicate who the sender is and who the typist was. (Sometimes this type of reference is placed not at the start but at the end of a letter, after the signatory). Alternatively, a reference number could relate to a numerical filing system within the office (see p. 118).

Date

The reference number is always followed by the date, either on the same line as the reference, but placed on the right-hand side of the paper, or on the left-hand side two lines below. It is best to write the date in figures and words: 15th December 1994, rather than 15.6.94. This is because in some languages (including American English) the day and the month are often written in a different order. For example, a French businessman fixes a meeting with a British client for 5.6.94. He arrives on 6th May, only to find that he is not expected until 5th June.

If you are punctuating the date, use the following formula: 15th December, 1994. If, however, you are using the open punctuation style, the date should read: 15 December 1994.

Americans write dates giving the month first (December 15, 1994), but this formula should be avoided in Britain.

Private/confidential

It may be that you are sending a personal letter to the addressee's place of work. In this case, you should mark the envelope, and place the word 'Private' as prominently as possible above the date. This means that the letter will not be opened by other members of staff, and if it is opened inadvertently the wording at the top of the letter should warn the reader not to continue reading.

The word 'Confidential' is used to describe a letter or document that contains sensitive information. Some managers and executives keep letters marked confidential to themselves, whereas others trust certain staff members with them. Thus, letters marked 'confidential' achieve a restricted circulation in the office.

Method of delivery

If you are putting your letter into recorded, registered or special delivery, or if you are using any other special means of carriage (courier, by hand, etc.), this should also be indicated after the date. If you are faxing a letter, the words 'Fax – Urgent' followed by the receiving fax number could also be placed here. However, there is no need to do this if you are using a front sheet (see p. 19).

Inside address

The inside address is crucial to the safe arrival of a business letter with the right person. It is not necessary to give an inside address in a personal/informal letter.

The inside address should be placed at the left-hand side of the letter, after the date, with each successive line flush against the left margin. It is wise to give the full address here as it is written on the outside of the envelope. If a letter goes astray, it may be possible to deduce its whereabouts by checking the file copy of the letter.

As far as possible, try to find out the name of the person who can deal with the matter at hand. Be sure to use the correct spelling of their name (find out their initials or first name, but use initials only in the inside address). If the addressee is a woman, find out whether she prefers Miss, Mrs or Ms. Note down also the addressee's exact title and department. The company's switchboard operator should be able to help you with these details.

Having the right name is important for a number of reasons. First, it helps you get things done quickly (a badly directed letter could spend weeks doing the rounds of an understaffed office before someone decides to take responsibility for your query or complaint). Having the right name also enables you to chase up the right person by telephone if you do not receive a satisfactory reply within a reasonable time. Finally, taking the trouble to find out the correct spelling and title shows courtesy and respect.

It is usual when addressing letters to banks, firms of solicitors and some other bodies to address only the company. Previous correspondence will tell you how to address your letter (banks, for example, usually ask on their letterhead that you address the Manager), or you can find out by calling the company in question.

Attention line

If you are addressing the company only, you may wish to add an 'attention line' at the start of the address, however, and this should be positioned two lines above the company name with a line space in between. The attention line, which is usually written 'Attn: Mr G. Brooks', for example, will indicate that there has been previous correspondence on this matter, dealt with by Mr Brooks.

It is always a good idea to follow the name with the person's position in the company. The person to whom you are writing may have left the company, or been transferred or promoted. If you give the position, your letter is less likely to be redirected to the addressee at her new company or in her newly exalted capacity. Instead, the letter will be passed to the person who now holds the post and can be dealt with more quickly.

(Pages 30-31 gives the items to include in an address, and pp. 94-6 gives details on using 'Mr', 'Esq.' and 'Mrs', 'Miss' or 'Ms'.)

Salutation

With the exception of postcards, memos, invitations and replies to invitations, all letters should start with a salutation: Dear Sir, Dear Mrs Briggs, Sir. The formality with which you open a letter depends on the relationship between you and the recipient. In choosing which formula to use, especially with people you have never met, try to strike a balance between stuffiness and over-familiarity. Your choice of salutation will also have bearing on your complimentary close (see p. 34).

The simple 'Sir' or 'Madam' is the most formal of all salutations. It is rarely used today, except perhaps in letters to the editors of national newspapers (see p. 303). 'Dear Sir' or 'Dear Madam' is used when you have not been given the name of the person to whom you are writing, when writing to a company rather than a person, or when the letter is very formal. For example, a job advertisement may ask for letters of application to be addressed to 'The Personnel Officer'. If this is the case, try to find out his or her name. If this fails, the 'Dear Sir or Madam' formula is best. Never write 'Dear Personnel Officer'.

If you know the name of the person you are writing to, it is usual to use their title and full name: Dear Mrs Briggs, Dear

Mr Jones. Do not use initials in a salutation of this type, reserve them for the inside address.

Some companies use the full name and omit the title: Dear Jennifer Briggs, Dear Andrew Jones. Although this means that you do not have to find out the addressee's preference on title, it has a feeling about it of pomposity or curtness. Many people are irritated by this practice, so avoid it if you can.

In the last three decades or so, business life has become much more informal. There was a time when even close colleagues addressed each other according to seniority, and no-one ever dared to call the boss by his Christian name. However, it is now quite common for co-workers and contacts in other companies to use each other's Christian names. If you have worked with a particular supplier for a number of years, you may well be on first-name terms, and it would be strange not to reflect this in your correspondence. But do so with care. There are still a large number of people out there who expect to be addressed formally, especially if they are thirty or forty years older than you are. Salutations for letters written to royalty or other titled people are sometimes extremely complicated. For guidance, see the list on pp. 99-106.

Subject heading

Most business letters begin with a subject heading, underlined or otherwise distinguished from the rest of the text. It should indicate the general subject of the letter for quick reference. It should sum up accurately in no more than two or three words what it is you are writing about. It may be a bank account number, the name of a project or company, or simply 'Your letter 25th August 1995'. Many people use 'Re:' at the start of a subject heading. This is an abbreviation of a Latin word, and should be avoided. Positioning the subject heading so that it acts as a title means you do not need to use 'Re:'.

Body of the letter

In general, the shorter the letter, the better. The first paragraph should tell the recipient why you are writing. The following paragraphs elaborate, and the final paragraph should sum up and elicit a response. If you need to give detailed information, it is best to do this on a separate sheet with a suitable heading, and attach it to your letter as an enclosure. For advice on how to plan and organize a letter see **Planning a Communication** pp. 41-9.

Subscription

There are many forms of subscription (which is also known as the complimentary close), and like salutations, the one you choose depends on the level of familiarity or formality between you and the addressee: to close a letter to an aunt 'Yours faithfully' would convey a formality that may suggest a falling-out. On the other hand, it would be very strange indeed to end a strongly-worded letter of complaint to a noisy neighbour with 'Kind regards'.

One rule exists to make things simpler: when using the 'Dear Sir'/'Dear Madam' salutation, always use 'Yours faithfully'. When writing to a person you have met or spoken to a number of times on the telephone, use 'Yours sincerely'. Other rules apply to subscriptions for letters to royalty, and these are dealt with in **Addressing an Envelope** pp. 98-102

Remember to match the subscription with the salutation and you can't go far wrong.

Signature

Signatures are normally made up of initials and surname, but may be simply the Christian name if the letter is personal and/or informal. When typing, six carriage returns should give you enough vertical space to fit in a signature.

SOME SUBSCRIPTIONS AND SOME SUGGESTIONS FOR USE

Yours faithfully	In business letters beginning 'Dear Sir'
Yours sincerely	To a business correspondent you have met or spoken with
Yours truly	As above, but going out of fashion now
Your obedient servant	Only used when addressing people of a certain rank (see pp. 102-3)
Sincerely	To a friend or relation in a formal letter (e.g., bereavement, thanks for hospitality, etc.)
Regards	A quick message to a neighbour, relative or close colleague
With kind regards	A neighbour, close business colleague of long standing
With best wishes	As above, but perhaps on a special occasion; also to less close relations
With love	A close family-member, lover, close friend
All my love	As above
Love from	To a child
Ever yours	A lover

Sometimes, the sender of a letter is not available to sign it once it has been typed. In this instance it is usual for the person responsible for typing the letter to put the letters 'pp' (meaning *per procurationem*, for and on behalf of) next to the signatory (the typed version of the sender's name – see overleaf) and to sign himself.

Signatory and designation

This is the typed version of the sender's signature, and gives either the full name or initials and surname. If the sender is a woman, then she should also have her preferred title (Mrs, Miss or Ms) typed in brackets after her name. The name should be followed by the sender's position in the company, typed on the line below. This is known as the designation, and it can add weight and authority to your words, but is most useful in that it enables your correspondent to get further letters and telephone calls through to you with the minimum of fuss.

If the letter is handwritten and formal, it is still a good idea to add your name in block capitals after your signature in the position where the signatory would normally be typed, and to give your preferred title in brackets.

Enclosures

If you are enclosing other materials along with your letter, indicate this by typing the abbreviation 'Enc.' or 'Encs' after the designation. Some people also give details of what the enclosures are, for extra information.

Copies

If a copy of the letter is being sent to another person, the abbreviation 'cc' is used to indicate this, followed by the name of the recipient(s) of the copy or copies. Some companies also send 'blind copies' to relevant people. These are not listed on the letter to the addressee, but will be labelled 'bc' on the sending office's file copy.

Continuation sheets

If you have to use more than one sheet of paper for your letter, it is informative to mark the first sheet with a catchword in the bottom right-hand corner, such as PTO, MORE, or CONTIN-UES. Continuation sheets should be numbered (although it is not necessary to number the letterhead), and the name of the addressee along with his or her company should be typed at the top of each new sheet on the left-hand side.

Component parts for informal letters

The guidelines given above are generally only followed strictly in business correspondence. Writers of informal and personal letters may bend the rules almost as much as they like. However, most informal letters still contain the following components:

- Sender's address (with telephone number if using printed stationery, without if handwriting the address).
- Salutation (except for instances such as postcards).
- Complimentary close.
- Signature.

Sample Letters

The sample letters on the following pages (pp. 38-40) show how to lay out all the component parts in semi-blocked and fully blocked style.

Example of semi-blocked layout, typed

15 The Elms,
Braunton,
GS22 4HB

26th June 1994

Mrs J. Pickford,
Manager,
Derryvale Hotel,
16 Holgate Street,
Derryvale,
DV2 7KG

Dear Mrs Pickford,

<u>Reservation</u>

Following our telephone conversation earlier today, please would you reserve a double room for my husband and me, for Friday 15th July to Sunday 17th July inclusive (2 nights bed and breakfast).

I understand the cost will be £40 per night, breakfast included.

I am enclosing a cheque for £20 as a non-refundable deposit against cancellation.

I look forward to meeting you.

Yours sincerely,

E. Bloggs (Mrs)
Enc.

Example of semi-blocked layout, handwritten

15 The Elms,
Braunton,
GS22 4HB

12th May 1994

Dear Mary and Andrew,
Congratulations – you've tied the knot at last! I was so glad to

see your picture in the paper. You both looked very happy, and
I hope that will continue.
　　Good luck, and congratulations once again.
　　　　　　　　　Best regards,
　　　　　　　　　　Liz

Example of fully-blocked layout, typed

　　　　　　　　　　　　　　　　　　2 The Cottages
　　　　　　　　　　　　　　　　　　Green Lane
　　　　　　　　　　　　　　　　　　London
　　　　　　　　　　　　　　　　　　SW24 8NG

21 August 1994

The Manager
Devonshire Bank
12 Market Street
Henton
GV22 6DE

Dear Sir

Personal accounts 0234567 & 0456723
Michael Dean and I have just got married. We both hold personal accounts at your branch. We would like to close our separate accounts and at the same time open a joint account. Please
would you let me know how best to do this, and send us any
forms necessary.

In view of our changed status, we both also need to review our
pensions. Do you have any information on pensions particularly
suitable for young married couples? If so we would be very glad
to receive it.

Yours faithfully

Jeanette Dean (nee Baker)

Example of fully-blocked layout with letterhead

X-Products Limited
15-17 High Street
Cumberley
CB1 9XY
Telephone 6996 0000
Fax 6996 0001

JB0149

15 November 1994

The Manager
Gregory's Restaurant
Plymouth Alley
Cumberley
CB1 4ED

Dear Sir

Christmas Catering
Our company is looking for a restaurant to cater for our staff
Christmas party on an evening in the week of Christmas Eve.

Please let me know whether you would be prepared to cater for
a party of about 25. I would be grateful if you would also send
details of any special set menu you are planning for Christmas,
price per head and your deposit requirements.

Yours faithfully

J Bloggs (Ms)
Company Secretary

JB/ds

- The reference can be placed *either* at the top or the bottom
  of the letter as shown in the above example.

PLANNING A COMMUNICATION

So far, this survey of practical techniques has dealt with the physical side of letter-writing: the kinds of paper to use, and the ways in which it is usual to lay out a letter. But what most people find difficult about writing is finding something to say, and organizing that material into a coherent whole. This problem often leads to procrastination ('I'm sorry I haven't written for more than five years ...'), or to writer's block (that feeling of not knowing how to start). Both of these could be fatal, and doubly so in the business context. Bad letters and bad letter-writers are bad for business

This chapter looks at ways to define, plan and draft an effective communication. The advice given will help those who simply do not know where to start, as well as those who are confronted with writing complex letters and have difficulty organizing the information. The process described will enable the letter-writer to perform the task more quickly and efficiently – a definite benefit, especially in business, where many letters need to be drafted each day. And by getting the message across efficiently, it will enable business to progress at the fastest possible pace.

Thorough planning is as important in letter-writing as it is in running a business or organizing an event. The main objects in planning a letter are to:

- Define the purpose of the communication.
- Collect all relevant information.
- Organize the information so that the reader can follow it.
- Ensure effective communication through appropriate language.

Purpose

All planning starts from a purpose. Have you ever tried shopping at a large supermarket without having first thought what meals you need to shop for? The normal result is a doubling of the length of time spent shopping as you cruise the aisles looking for inspiration, and coming home missing at least one essential item. In extreme cases, the shopper comes home with nothing at all of use. Writing a shopping list, or just thinking in advance about the meals being shopped for, would ensure that less time is spent in the supermarket feeling confused and irritated. The shopper may also succeed in coming home with every item he or she needs.

There may be as many reasons for writing a letter as there are dinners to be cooked. If the writer does not know why he or she is putting pen to paper, how is the job to be done without wasting time, and how can the writer avoid missing out essential ingredients? Furthermore, if the writer does not know the reason for writing, how is the recipient to respond with the appropriate action?

In general, letters fall into one or more of the following categories of function:

- To request information.
- To pass on information.
- To request or recommend that an action be taken.
- To pass on news.
- To pass on a message of congratulations/condolence/etc.

The first step in putting together a letter is to decide which category it falls into. A letter to the bank may be a request for information ('please send me details of your share-dealing service'), or a request for action ('please let me know when we could meet to discuss my account').

Some letters combine one or more of the above functions. A recommendation of action may need to be backed up with information, for example. A letter of thanks for a birthday present may simply pass on a message of gratitude, or it may go further and convey news as well.

It is useful to spend a few minutes considering the purpose of your letter, and then jot it down. This statement is the basis of the plan for the letter.

Collecting and organizing information

The statement of purpose is useless on its own. It now needs to be made specific by deciding what information is necessary to fulfil the stated purpose of the letter. You will need to jot down:

- The name, address and position of the person to whom you are writing.
- A statement of why you were prompted to write (a previous letter from the correspondent? a telephone conversation? a recommendation from a third party?).
- A statement of what you expect the recipient to do when they receive your letter (send information? perform some action?).
- A list of the points of information you wish to convey to enable the recipient to respond as you require.

The last point on the above list is probably the most difficult to formulate, especially if the letter needs to contain a lot of information organized into an argument of some sort.

At this early stage, simply jot down at random the points you wish to make. Make notes of facts and figures your reader may need, but which you cannot immediately supply, and spend time looking for them. According to surveys, a large proportion of business time is wasted requesting and sending information, which could have been given in the first place, and clarifying points that were explained badly. This is a terrible waste of time and money, and can be avoided by careful thought at the start.

When planning the letter, always keep the reader in mind.

What does she need to know to respond quickly and effective-ly? Is there any information missing? What is your relation-ship with her (very formal, formal, informal, very close)?

First draft

After the purpose of the letter has been defined and all rele-vant information has been collected, it is time to make a first, rough draft. This can be handwritten, and can be built up according to the following stages:

- Opening. The first line or paragraph, which indicates what prompted you to write and the reason for writing.
- Body of the letter. A number of paragraphs setting out information or an argument, or just separate pieces of 'news'. If you are tempted to write any more than, say, four paragraphs in this stage, you may consider moving the information to an attached report.
- Close. The last paragraph, in which you state clearly the response you are expecting, and when you need to hear from the reader.

Openings

Do not waste valuable time with an opening that states the obvious:

'I am writing in response to your advert ...'
'We are in receipt of your letter, which we received at this office today.'
'Just a note to say...'

Of course you are writing, of course the letter has been received at that office, or that office would not be responding. And yes, it is 'just a note' – you obviously could not be bothered to write a full letter! Try:

> 'I saw your advertisement in yesterday's *Daily Press* and would like to apply for the job...'
> 'Thank you for your letter of 25th April.'
> 'I am enclosing the information you requested...'

These are good openings that get straight to the heart of the matter. Here are some more examples:

> 'Thank you for your enquiry about ... I am enclosing the information ...'
> 'As discussed in our telephone conversation yesterday, I am sending ...'
> 'I would like to apply for the position of ... which I saw advertised in ...'
> 'It was good to meet you yesterday...'
> 'Thank you for taking the time to meet with me last week ...'
> 'I was so sorry to hear ...'
> 'Mr Bloggs suggested that I contact you with regard to ...'
> 'I have been referred to you by...'
> 'I wish to recommend ...'
> 'I wish to make a complaint ...'

If these openings or ones like them are used, the reader will understand your purpose immediately, avoiding the need to muddle through reams of information before finding out why you are writing.

The formality of the opening will depend on your relationship with the correspondent, and should reflect the same level as the salutation and complimentary close (see pp. 32 and 34).

The body of the letter

Organize the information you have jotted down into an order

45

that follows a logical train of thought from start to finish. Most people usually give the most important points first, and place the rest of the information in order of declining importance. This is particularly important if you think that the reader needs to be persuaded in the first paragraph or he will lose interest.

If you are drafting a letter that requires an argument, it may be useful to go through an intermediate planning stage before you start stringing words together. Do this by taking your random notes, numbering them according to the order in which they will appear, and make notes on the connections between each point. This will enable you to move from one point to another showing the reader clearly your reasoning. **Grammar and Style** (pp. 81-3) gives advice on using connecting words and sentences.

Closing paragraph

This paragraph is one of the most important in the letter. It is the point at which you draw a conclusion and make a clear statement of the action you require and the timescale involved, for example:

'I would therefore be grateful if you would send me all the information you have on the bank's share-dealing service as soon as possible.'

'With this in mind, it is important that we meet in the next two or three days. I would be grateful if you would call to arrange a time.'

Both of these endings request an action and give a timescale. They both also make reference back to the information given in the body of the letter, to show the connection between the two.

Pause for thought

If your letter is an important and complex one, it is a good idea to leave the draft overnight, or from morning until the afternoon, before beginning to make the final version. Many people find that stronger arguments or further points of information occur to them as time passes, and they would have no opportunity to add them to the letter if it was already sealed and sent.

When you come to writing or typing the final version, you will need to add all those elements of laying out a letter mentioned in **Layout and Component Parts** (pp. 26-40). Check through the draft with the following questions in mind:

- Am I addressing the right person – is he or she in a position to act on its contents?
- Do I have the correct spelling of the name, the correct title and the full address?
- Is the salutation appropriate to my relationship with the addressee? (See pp. 32-3.)
- Can I find a succinct subject heading to sum up the contents of the letter? (See p. 33.)
- Is the opening straightforward, and does it accurately reflect my reason for writing?
- Are the points of information or argument given in the body of the letter put clearly, and in the correct order? (See **Grammar and Style** pp. 73-90.)
- Have I given all the information necessary for the recipient to carry out the action I require?
- Have I given information that is not relevant, and which could be removed?
- Is the letter too long for the information to be digested easily? Could I separate out the information into a report/list, and send it as an enclosure?
- Have I used the final paragraph to state clearly the response I require, and a timescale?

- Does the complimentary close (see pp. 34-5) reflect my relationship with the addressee, and correspond with the salutation?
- Is the English easy to read and without spelling errors and tortuous sentence constructions? (See pp. 50-90.)
- Do I have all the necessary enclosures?
- Am I using the writing materials appropriate to the context?

When all these questions are answered satisfactorily, the letter can finally be typed and sent on its way.

Saving time

Business thrives on communication, and despite advances in electronic communications, the letter is still the most popular way to get a message across. Facsimile transmissions are most often made in the form of letters, and important telephone conversations and meetings are still confirmed in writing. Thus, many businesses devote a fair proportion of staff time to drafting and typing letters.

It may be possible to save time by using previous letters as a standard pattern, and simply changing relevant details, especially for circumstances that are similar and frequently arise: requests for information/price lists/brochures/etc., are a good example. Many word-processing packages enable staff to send the same letter to many people, by changing only certain details, such as the name, address and date. Unless this is painfully obvious to the recipient from the format of the letter, there aren't many people who object to receiving 'processed' responses to routine enquiries.

Any scheme that saves time drafting routine letters is a good idea. However, one pitfall is that staff become blasé. They fail to read incoming mail correctly, or they send out a standard letter that doesn't quite fit the circumstances instead of taking the time to add those few extra words. Either way the company has egg on its face, and may well lose custom as a result.

So keep an eye on the standard letters that are on file. Take care to update and amend them to fit the situation precisely, and try always to improve the wording for future use. Above all, never send a routine response to an enquiry that demands your personal attention.

Spending time planning and drafting a letter is a rewarding process. It may seem as if it cuts into the working day unnecessarily, but a single letter that gets an immediate result is better by far than a confused letter that requires a number of correspondences before the recipient is certain what you are asking for, or can act on the information.

A short letter that is clear in its aims will prompt the recipient to immediate action. A long rambling missive may be left for days in the pending tray until the recipient can find enough time and motivation to unravel your thought processes. It may even go completely unanswered.

A well-written letter is desirable because it is effective.

PUNCTUATION AND SPELLING

Correct spelling and punctuation are the tools to be used when producing any piece of writing. Without a mastery of spelling and punctuation writing of any kind becomes laborious, and it is difficult to be sure that your correspondent will understand your message. At the same time, correct spelling and punctuation are seen as signs of a person's efficiency and reliability.

The elements of punctuation

Punctuation is used to separate words into groups in order to make their meaning clear. The 'weapons' in the punctuation 'armoury', when used according to their proper function, can enable the writer to make complex sentences without losing the reader's interest or understanding. Wrong punctuation, on the other hand, can in some cases lead to ambiguity and error.

Full stop (.)

The full stop is used to mark the end of a sentence. It is also used to show that a word has been abbreviated. Abbreviations are those words that have been shortened so that they do not include the last letter of the original word. Contractions, on the other hand, are shortened words that do contain the last letter of the word. Contractions do not need a full stop:

- Dr = Doctor (contraction, therefore no full stop).
- Mr = Mister (contraction, therefore no full stop).
- Mrs = Mistress (contraction, therefore no full stop).
- p.m. = post meridiem (abbreviations, therefore use full stops).
- P.O. = Post Office (abbreviations, therefore use full stops).

In the UK and the USA, a full stop is also used to mark the decimal point. However, in many countries, including most of those in Continental Europe, the full stop is replaced by a comma in this context.

Comma (,)

A comma is used to separate one part of a sentence (clause) from another. It marks a short pause for breath:

'Aunt Molly said she would think about coming at Christmas, but we have not heard from her yet.'

'Although we have not heard from her yet, we are expecting Aunt Molly for Christmas.'

If the clause can be removed from the sentence without changing its basic meaning, use two commas, one at the start and one at the end of the clause, to mark it off:

'The information pack, which I read over the weekend, has been very instructive.'

The clause between the commas must relate to the subject of the sentence (in the above case, 'the information pack'). (See p. 86.)

Commas are also used to separate items in a list:

'Jane has now passed grades one, two, three and four in music.'

Note there is no comma before the word 'and' in English. Writers of American English frequently put a comma in this position (when it is known as the 'serial comma'), but it is not usual in the UK.

Semi-colon (;)

This is used to mark a pause that is not quite as long as a full stop. The two parts of a sentence separated by a semi-colon are usually linked in some way:

'The night shift staff start appearing at about 4.15 p.m.; the day shift ends at 4.30 p.m.'

A semi-colon is also used to separate items in a list where those items are long enough to include commas. This avoids confusion with the comma, which would normally be used. If semi-colons are used in a list, the start of the list is normally marked with a colon:

'We have visited so many places in the last few days: Montmartre, where artists sell their work on the streets; the Georges Pompidou Centre, with its weird modern architecture; the beautiful Notre Dame Cathedral; and of course, the Eiffel Tower.'

Colon (:)

The colon is used to mark the start of a list (as above), but also to separate two parts of a sentence where the second half illustrates a statement made in the first half.

'This nation remains divided: rich and poor, north and south, the employed and the unemployed.'

Apostrophe (')

Used to indicate the possessive or to show that some letters have been omitted from a word:

'It's Julian's day off.'

In this sentence, the apostrophe is used in two different ways:

in the words 'it's', it shows that a letter is missing (it is). In 'Julian's', the apostrophe indicates that the day off belongs to Julian.

While it is usual to add an apostrophe to a noun to make it possessive (Julian becomes Julian's), do not add the apostrophe when using the pronoun: his, hers, theirs, its, ours, yours. The exception to this rule is 'one's'.

When making a possessive from an English name that ends in 's', a decision needs to be made about whether to add the second 's' or whether to add just the apostrophe (Mr Jones's, for example). It is normal to add the second 's', but if pronunciation would be awkward (e.g. Mr Bridges's), omit it (Mr Bridges').

With Greek and Biblical names (e.g. Archimedes' principle), and phrases containing the word 'sake' (for heavens' sake, for conscience' sake), it is usual to omit the second 's'. If you are unsure what to do it may be a good idea to avoid the problem altogether by turning the phrase around and inserting the word 'of' (e.g. for appearance' sake becomes for the sake of appearance).

GETTING IT RIGHT

One of the most common mistakes made in written English is misuse of these two tiny words. It even appears in advertising and on shop signs.

Its means 'belonging to it.'
It's is a shortened form of 'it is.'

Inverted commas (' ') and quotation marks (" ")

Single inverted commas are used to show that a word is being used to mean something slightly different from usual, or to indicate a slang word. Use inverted commas where you might otherwise use 'so-called'.

His so-called skills in letter-writing are non-existent.
His 'skills' in letter-writing are non-existent.

Inverted commas are also used to show that the words inside them are being quoted:

She said, 'His so-called skills in letter-writing are non-existent'.

The full stop is placed outside the closing inverted comma because the quoted section forms only part of the sentence. If the sentence included only the quotation, the full stop would be placed inside the closing inverted comma:

'His so-called skills in letter-writing are non-existent.'

Quotation marks are used to indicate a quote within a quote:

'This card says "Get Well Soon",' she said.

Exclamation mark (!)

This punctuation mark is used to round off an exclamation (a sharp command: Get out!, Go away!, Come here!). It should not be used to add excitement to a simple statement or to punctuate a joke.

Question mark (?)

The question mark is used in place of a full stop at the end of a question. It is now sometimes also used instead of semi-colons (see p. 52) to mark a list of questions.

Brackets ( ) or [ ]

Brackets are used to mark off parts of a sentence that are extra, much in the same way as commas are used to mark off subordinate clauses (see p. 86). They can also be used to enclose abbreviations, definitions, examples and illustrations, and numbers in lists:

'International Business Machines (IBM) declared profits of ...'
'IBM (the computer giant) declared profits of ...'
'IBM (which employs 2,000 staff in the town) declared profits of ...'
'I cannot come to see you (1) because I can't afford the fare, (2) because I am very busy and (3) because I am on call every weekend.'

Like double quotation marks, square brackets ([ ]) are most often used to mark a parenthesis within round brackets. They are sometimes also used when a word or phrase is introduced into a quotation so that it makes sense when taken out of context:

'Perhaps the only good thing [about taking a holiday at this time] is the absence of crowds of tourists.'

There are also a number of technical uses in fields such as mathematics.

Dash (–)

A dash is an informal method of marking a parenthesis, in a similar way to a pair of commas or brackets. It gives a pause that is slightly longer than a comma but shorter than a semicolon. It should be written with a single space on either side of it. Some DTP systems are able to give two lengths of dash. The longer is the width of the letter 'm' (known as an em-dash), and the shorter is the width of the letter 'n' (an en-dash). The hyphen (see below) is shorter again than the en-dash.

Hyphen (-)

This short line is used to show that a word has been 'broken' from one line of text to the next, or to separate suffixes such as re- from nouns where they would otherwise cause confusion:

- recreation means play, but re-creation means creating again
- recover means get well, but re-cover means covering again
- reform means to reorganize, but re-form means to form anew.

Hyphens are also used for a whole host of other reasons, mostly to string two or more separate words together into one idea, or to show a relationship:

- bargain-hunting
- labour-saving device
- a twelve-year-old child
- follow-up
- East-West relations = relations between East and West
- 50–60% = between 50 and 60%.

Capital letters

Capitals should be used in the following instances:

- At the start of a sentence.
- At the start of proper nouns (people, places, organizations, etc.).

- For the titles of things (books, plays, songs, etc.).
- In some abbreviations, and always in acronyms.
- For the word 'I'.
- For certain words connected to religion – God (when referring to the one God, and not many gods), the Bible, the Qur'an, Allah, etc.
- For titles of people, when referring to the title holder, but not when referring to the title itself: 'He became president of the USA' but 'I saw that President Clinton had already arrived' and 'I saw that the President had already arrived'.

Bullets (•)

These black dots are available on word-processing software, and can be used to mark items in a list, as in this book, especially where each item in the list runs to more than one line.

Spelling it right

Most word-processing packages now include an electronic dictionary and spell-checker, and a large number of people rely on them alone to ensure that letters contain no errors of spelling. However, spell-check programmes are fallible, and are no alternative to the power of the human brain.

Most spelling errors occur simply as a slip of the pen or typist's finger. However, some people really do have difficulty recognizing words that are spelled incorrectly, and this can be a serious handicap, especially if called upon to write business letters. You may be perfectly well-qualified in your field, but if you frequently make spelling mistakes, some people may begin to doubt your competence.

Spelling ability can be improved very quickly by doing some or all of the following:

- Read as much as you can. This will help you to recognize misspelled words, and help to improve your writing style overall (see **Grammar and Style** pp. 73-90).

- If you have time, slow your reading right down so that you can say each word under your breath. Say each syllable carefully and look at how long words are constructed.
- Ask a friend to give you dictation (you could also record passages onto a dictaphone). Read through your work and check each word. If there are words you have misspelled, make a list and learn them.
- Always check words you are unsure of in a dictionary
- Make a large notice of a word you always have trouble spelling. Hang it by a mirror or over the kitchen sink, and read it every day.
- Always read through letters you have written, looking for spelling mistakes and words you have missed out. Don't rely on a computer to help you.

The rest of this section contains three lists of words. The first is a list of words that a spell-check programme may skip over as correct, because they are words in themselves, but used in the wrong context (knot for not, four instead of for, too instead of to or two). Such words are known as homonyms. The second lists commonly misspelled plurals, and the third is a list of other words that are frequently misspelled.

Homonyms and other words your spell-checker may miss

adverse (bad)	averse (does not like)
affect (to influence)	effect (*noun*, a result; *verb*, to put into action)
accept (to receive)	except (make an exception)
ail *see* ale	
air *see* heir	
aisle (part of a church)	isle (island)
ale (beer)	ail (become sick)

allowed (permitted)	aloud (capable of being heard)
ant (insect)	aunt (female relative)
anti (against)	ante (before)
assure *see* ensure	
ate (past tense eat)	eight (7+1)
aunt *see* ant	
averse *see* adverse	
aye *see* eye	
bad (not good)	bade (commanded)
bail (money to go free/to empty [a boat])	bale (of hay)
ball (toy)	bawl (scream)
bare (naked)	bear (brown and furry/to carry)
bawl *see* ball	
beach (by the sea)	beech (type of tree)
bear *see* bare	
beech *see* beach	
bell (rings)	belle (beautiful girl)
blew (what the wind does)	blue (colour)
boar (fierce pig)	bore (drill/make bored)
board *see* bored	
bore *see* boar	
bored (be tired of)	board (flat, stiff material)
bough (branch)	bow (like curtsey/front of boat)
boy (young man)	buoy (float)
business (a company)	busyness (being busy)
buy (purchase)	by (near); bye (good-bye)
canvas (cloth)	canvass (seek opinions/votes)
ceiling (above your head)	sealing (closing firmly)
cellar (basement)	seller (person who sells)
cereal *see* serial	
cheap (not expensive)	cheep (sound of a bird)
check (look at again)	cheque (drawn on the bank)
cheep *see* cheap	

cheque *see* check

coarse (rough) course (as in racecourse)

complement (to complete) compliment (to praise)

core (centre) corps (body of people)

council (group of people) counsel (give advice)

course *see* coarse

cruise (to sail) crews (ships' staff)

currant (fruit) current (flow/the immediate present)

dear (loved) deer (the animal)

decease *see* disease

deer *see* dear

dependent (influenced by) dependant (person who depends on something)

desert (arid place) dessert (pudding)

device (machine) devise (to plan)

diner (a person who eats/ a restaurant) dinner (the meal)

disease (illness) decease (die)

draft (first try) draught (mouthful, breeze)

dual (double) duel (ritual fight)

effect *see* affect

eight *see* ate

elicit (to draw out) illicit (secret, illegal)

eligible *see* illegible

emigrant (leaves the country) immigrant (enters the country)

eminent (famous) imminent (immediate); immanent (inherent)

enquire (to ask) inquire (to investigate)

ensure (to make sure) (give assurances) insure (to protect against); assure

exalt (to praise highly) exult (to be joyful)

except *see* accept

excrete (to discharge)	execrate (to detest)
exercise (to keep fit)	exorcise (evil spirits)
eye (to see with)	aye (yes)
fain (willingly)	feign (pretend)
faint (lose consciousness)	feint (faint lines, distracting movement)
fiend *see* friend	
forward (in front)	foreword (preface)
friend (pal)	fiend (devil)
hear (a sound)	here (not there)
heir (beneficiary to a will	air (we breathe)
here *see* hear	
hole (cavity)	whole (complete)
hour *see* our	
illegible (unreadable)	eligible (fit to be chosen)
illicit *see* elicit	
immanent *see* eminent	
immigrant *see* emigrant	
imminent *see* eminent	
inquire *see* enquire	
insure *see* ensure	
isle *see* aisle	
it's (it is)	its (belonging to it)
knew *see* new	
knot *see* not	
know *see* no	
knows *see* nose	
lead *see* led	
leant *see* lent	
led (past tense to lead)	lead (present tense to lead/heavy metal)
lent (gave on loan)	leant (past tense to lean)
lightening (making lighter)	lightning (thunder and ...)
loan (money leant)	lone (alone)

lose (to misplace) — loose (not tight)
made (created) — maid (young woman)
meter (measuring device) — metre (100 centimetres)
new (not old) — knew (was aware of)
no (negative) — know (to be aware of)
nose (on your face) — knows (is aware of)
not (negative) — knot (tied in a rope)
of (belonging to) — off (not on)
one *see* won
our (belonging to us) — hour (part of the day)
pail (bucket) — pale (white)
pain (ache) — pane (sheet of glass)
pale *see* pail
pane *see* pain
passed (passed by) — past (historical)
peace (not war) — piece (part of)
personal (private) — personnel (staff)
picture (drawing) — pitcher (jug)
piece *see* peace
pitcher *see* picture
practice (custom) — practise (to rehearse)
precede (go before) — proceed (move on)
principle (rule) — principal (primary/chief)
proceed *see* precede
rain (wet stuff) — rein (for a horse); reign (period of rule)
read (a book) — reed (plant growing in water)
review (look over again) — revue (cabaret show)
right (not wrong) — write (put pen to paper); rite (ritual)
route (itinerary) — rout (retreat); root (of a plant)
scene (view) — seen (past tense to see)
sealing *see* ceiling
seem (appear to be) — seam (a join)

seen *see* scene
seller *see* cellar

serial (story told in parts)	cereal (foodstuff)
so (as a result)	sew (with needle and thread)
son (boy-child)	sun (in the sky)
stationery (envelopes)	stationary (not moving)
steal (take by theft)	steel (the metal)
story (tale)	storey (floor of a building)

sun *see* son

tears (weeping)	tiers (levels)
there (not here)	their (belonging to them); they're (they are)

tiers *see* tears
tire *see* tyre

to (towards/e.g. to do)	two (1+1); too (also/excessive)
tyre (runner cushion)	tire (become fatigued)
waist (above the hips)	waste (not use)
wait (for a bus)	weight (in stones and pounds)
waive (not to claim)	wave (a life on the ocean ...)

waste *see* waist
wear *see* where
weather *see* whether
weight *see* wait

where (in what place)	wear (e.g. wear clothes/wear out)
whether (if)	weather (rain, sun, snow, etc.)

who's *see* whose
whole *see* hole

whose (belonging to whom)	who's (who is)
won (gained victory)	one (3 minus 2)
would (e.g. he would)	wood (product of a tree)

write *see* right

your (belonging to you)	you're (you are)

Some difficult plurals

aficionado	aficionados
alumnus	alumni
archipelago	archipelagos
brother-in-law	brothers-in-law
bureau	bureaux
cannon	no plural
cargo	cargoes
chateau	chateaux
chief	chiefs
circus	circuses
cupful	cupfuls
curriculum vitae	curricula vitae
deer	no plural
desperado	desperados
diary	diaries
dynamo	dynamos
echo	echoes
embargo	embargoes
embryo	embryos
focus	focuses
folio	folios
forum	forums
gas	gases
genius	geniuses
ghetto	ghettos
halo	haloes
hero	heroes
hoof	hoofs
innuendo	innuendoes
knife	knives
leaf	leaves
loaf	loaves

maid-of-honour	maids-of-honour
man-of-war	men-of-war
manifesto	manifestoes
memento	mementoes
mosquito	mosquitoes
motto	mottoes
no	noes
nucleus	nuclei
ox	oxen
passer-by	passers-by
phenomenon	phenomena
piano	pianos
plateau	plateaux
potato	potatoes
prospectus	prospectuses
proviso	provisoes
radio	radios
reef	reefs
referendum	referendums
roof	roofs
salvo	salvoes
sheep	no plural
sister-in-law	sisters-in-law
solo	solos
son-in-law	sons-in-law
spoonful	spoonfuls
stadium	stadiums
stimulus	stimuli
stratum	strata
terminus	termini
thief	thieves
tomato	tomatoes
tornado	tornadoes
torpedo	torpedoes

vacuum	vacuums
veto	vetoes
volcano	volcanoes

Some words have no singular, e.g.: scissors, trousers, tidings, thanks, spectacles.

Other commonly misspelled words

absorb, absorption
acknowledge, acknowledgment/acknowledgement
accidentally
accommodate, accommodation
achieve, achievement
acquaintance
acquire, acquisition
address, addressing, addressee
adequate
advertise, advertisement
aeroplane *not* airplane
agree, agreeing, agreeable
aggression
allot, allotted, allottment
amateur
among
analyse, analysis, analyses (plural)
anonymous
anxiety, anxious
apparent
appear, appearance
appropriate
arctic
argue, arguing, argument
atmosphere

attach, attached
awful, awfully
bachelor
beautiful, beautifully
believe
benefit, benefited
breathe
busy
careful, carefully
channel, channelled
character, characteristically
cigarette
colour
commemorate
commit, committed, committee, commitment
comparative, comparatively
complete, completely
conceive, conceivably
conscientious
conscious
damage, damaged, damaging
deceive, deceit
decide, decided, decision
defence, defensive
descend, descendant
desperate, desperately
detach, detached
deteriorate
develop, developed, development
diamond
diesel
disappear, disappeared, disappearance
disappoint, disappointment
disaster, disastrous

discipline
dissatisfied
disservice
dissuade
doubt
due, duly
dye, dyeing
eight, eighth
embarrass, embarrassment
excite, exciting, excitement
exercise
exhibition
exhilarating
expense, expensive, expensively
faithful, faithfully
February
finish, finished, finishing
foreign
forty
fourteen
fuel, fuelling
fulfil, fulfilled, fulfilment
grief, grievous, grievance
guarantee, guaranteed, guaranteeing
guide, guidance
half, halves
happen, happened
height
honest, honestly
humour, humorous
hygiene
identical, identically
illegal, illegally
illiterate, illiteracy

immediate, immediately
immense, immensely
inadequate
incidentally
incur, incurring
independent
indispensable
inoculate
install, instalment
irregular, irregularity
jeopardy, jeopardise
jewellery
knowledge, knowledgeable
label, labelled
language
leisure
liaise, liaison
library
likelihood
livelihood
maintain, maintenance
manage, manager, management
manoeuvre, manoeuvring
marry, marrying, marriage, married
messenger
minuscule
minute
miscellaneous
necessary
occur, occurred, occurring, occurrence
panic, panicked
parliament, parliamentary
peculiar, peculiarity
permit, permitted, permission, permissable

physical, physically
pleasant, pleasure
possess, possession
predecessor
prepare, preparation
previous
primary, primarily
proceed, procedure
profession, professional, professionally
pronounce, pronunciation
public, publicly
pursue, pursuing
quality
real, really
receive, receipt
recommend
reconnaisance
refer, referring, reference
regret, regretted
relevant
retrieve
rhythm
ridicule, ridiculous
routine
satisfied, dissatisfied
sacrilege, sacrilegious
scarce, scarcity, scarcely
science, scientific, scientifically
scissors
secret, secrecy
secretary
sentence
separate, separation
service, servicing, serviceable

severe, severely
similar, similarity, similarly
sincere, sincerely, sincerity
skill, skilful, skilfully
solicitor
special, specially
speech
statistics, statistically
straight, straighten
succeed, success, successful, successfully
sudden, suddenness
supervise, supervisor
surprise
syllabus
tariff
technique, technical, technically
temperature
temporary, temporarily
tobacco
tomorrow
traffic
truth, truly, truthfully
twelve, twelfth
typical
underrate
unnatural
unnecessary
until
usual, usually
vaccinate
valuable
various, variety
vehicle
view

visit, visited, visitor
Wednesday
weigh, weight
welcome
wise, wisely, wisdom
withhold
woman, women
yield

GRAMMAR AND STYLE

Spoken language combines the physical sounds of words with the identity and 'body language' (facial expression, body posture, gestures, etc.) of the person saying them, to produce a very complex message. Unless they are carefully scripted, conversations progress more by consensus ('I know what you mean') and a kind of intuition than by the accurate use of words in well-ordered sentences. Ironies are identified with a wry smile; emphasis or process is conveyed with a hand gesture; the relationship between each person is perceived through posture.

When it comes to communicating on paper, however, the physical side of that conversation is lost. Writers are reduced to words on paper. In some cases, they don't even know what their correspondent looks like, how old they are, or whether they are male or female. Because of this, language takes on a much more important role in the communication. Letter writers need to use the right words in the right order, so as to avoid ambiguity, but they must also somehow convey a feeling of who they are, and how they perceive their correspondent.

The basis of good writing is, of course, the use of the correct grammar. But there is more to natural style than just understanding the rules. This section gives some hints on good grammar, but also advises on how to write simply and effectively, and how to convey the correct messages in the most appropriate manner. It shows how to avoid using words and phrases that are meaningless, and how to divide the writing into rhythmic sentences and paragraphs that will be read attentively, and get you the result you want.

Choosing the right words

The English language contains a large number of words. It is a complex language because it makes many subtle distinctions between different types of thing, i.e. there are many words that mean almost the same thing as each other, but not quite. Choosing the right word can be a difficult task, and many people fall into the habit of using clichés or formula sentences that have been read so often that they are simply ignored as meaningless.

Use everyday words

As a rule in modern correspondence, use short, everyday words, unless a longer word is really the correct one. Brevity is always desirable, so if you find you can use one word instead of three, do so.

A TREASURY OF WORDS

An excellent investment is a thesaurus, particularly Roget's *Thesaurus*, which is a treasury of words divided by meaning and subject area. Use it for those times when you simply can't think of the right word, or have it teetering on the tip of your tongue. Use it also to find close synonyms to replace often-repeated words for variation.

Meaning

Never use words that you do not understand; if you use the wrong word, or show you are ignorant of its meaning, you run the risk of losing the respect of your correspondent. You may also cause time-wasting confusion into the bargain. A dictionary is a necessary reference for anyone who writes letters.

Never use a noun as a verb

This is a frequent fault among those who wish to make their style racy, particularly those in advertising. It creates ugly constructions that may be difficult to read (some people may even suspect a typing error), so avoid it. Look out for such sentences as 'It will impact our sales', and use the more usual construction 'It will make an impact on ...'.

Avoid tautologies

Tautologies are usually two- or three-word phrases that say the same thing twice: numerous in number; new innovation; advance planning. Some tautologies may even cause hilarity, and they can always be pared down. Probably the most famous tautology in the language at present relates to killing something dead.

Avoid euphemisms

A euphemism is a word used when a person is trying to skirt around the issue by not naming the subject. 'House of ill repute' is a euphemism for 'brothel', just as 'lady of the night' is a euphemism for 'prostitute'. Of course, euphemisms can add humour to a personal letter, but in the interests of directness and clarity in formal and business correspondence, it is best to avoid them.

Tempting phrases and their alternatives

This list gives a number of clichés, tautologies and other outmoded or faddish words and long-winded phrases that should be eradicated from modern correspondence. It also gives straightforward modern alternatives. Replacing these tempting phrases with pared-down alternatives may cut the length (and fuddle-factor) of a letter drastically.

Delete	Replace with
additionally	and
advance planning	planning
affirmative action	action
analogous to	similar to
at a later date	later
at the present time	now/currently
attached hereto	enclosed
bring to a close	end
bring to a conclusion	end
by means of	by
cater to	serve
consensus of opinion	consensus
costs an arm and a leg	is expensive/overpriced
due to the fact that	because
end result	result
fed up to the back teeth with	tired of
first and foremost	first
for a period	for
get cold feet	be cautious
has a tendency to	tends to
has an ability to	can
has no stomach for	does not want
hereinafter	after
hold a conference	confer
hold a meeting	meet
in close proximity to	close to/nearby
in connection with	about
in regard to	about
in the foreseeable future	soon
in the near future	soon
in the order of	approximately
in the region of	about/approximately
in-depth study	study

it has come to my attention	I notice
it is anticipated to be	I/we expect
it is necessary to	we/I must
last but not least	finally
like the palm of my hand	well
make a decision	decide
make an investigation of	investigate
make a recommendation	recommend
make contact with	meet/reach
more often than not	often
money down the drain	wasteful
new innovation	innovation
numerous in number	many
of the 13th inst	of 13th April (this month)
of the opinion that	believes
on a daily basis	daily/every day
on the part of	for
on two different occasions	twice
past history	history
persons	people
postponed until later	postponed
pursuant to	following/after
put your account in order	pay your bill/debt
range all the way from	range from
repeat again	repeat
resembling in nature	like
stick to his guns	persevere
stand in the way	prevent
subsequent to	after
take action	act
take into consideration	consider
that is to say	that is
the undersigned	I
until such time as	until

we acknowledge receipt of	thank you for
we are in receipt of	thank you for
with respect to	concerning

Either/or, neither/nor, not only/but

Here are three pairs of words that are often used incorrectly, they are often mixed up and used in the same sentence. However, they should only be used in their pairs.

'Either' and 'or' refer to a choice: 'I will take either the 5.30 or the 6.00 from Glasgow'.

'Neither' and 'nor' refer to two negatives: 'I will take neither the 5.30 nor the 6.00 from Glasgow'.

'Not only' and 'but' are used to compound one thing on another: 'He not only ignored me, but allowed the door to slam in my face'.

Sexist language

Using language that excludes people of either sex or any race is not only 'politically incorrect' – it could also be illegal, especially if published in any form. Therefore, practise using neutral words: police-officer, not policeman; postal worker, not postman; chair, rather than chairman. Try also to avoid using 'he' for every unspecific person. If you find it unwieldy to substitute 'he' with 'he/she', alternate the pronouns used. Remember that a 'he' can be an executive or a secretary, a nurse or a doctor, a parent, a teacher, a welder or a dressmaker; and so can a 'she' be all of these things.

Some general points of grammar

Grammar is essentially the mechanics of language. It names each part of a sentence and gives rules for their uses. Unhappily, modern educators do not seem to teach grammar to schoolchildren. So some people often find themselves in a situation similar to a driver whose car breaks down but has no idea what is wrong or how to fix it: they know a sentence is awkward or badly constructed, but have no idea why or how to solve the problem. Here are some rules that cover the most common grammatical problems.

Never end a sentence with a preposition

'This is a rule I would always adhere to.'

The writer here is plainly deluded. If he or she were to adhere to the rule above, the sentence would read: 'This is a rule to which I would always adhere.' The verb has taken the place of the preposition at the end of the sentence, which appears to be better balanced as a consequence.

However, it is a good idea to follow 'normal' word order (see p. 82), so an even better solution would be: 'I (subject) would always adhere (verb) to this rule (object).'

Never split the infinitive

This rule may be a cliché, but it still stands as a rule of good style, and should still be observed, unless there is a good reason for not doing so:

'To go boldly' not 'to boldly go'.

The number of the subject should equal the number of the verb

Always check that the subject tallies with the verb of the sentence. If the subject is singular, then the verb should be singular. If the subject is plural (two people, two things), then the verb should also be in the plural:

'Mr Judd and Ms Harris are expected to arrive at any minute.'

The above is a simple case – plural subject (Mr Judd and Ms Harris), plural verb (they are expected).

However, problems might arise when the number of the subject is not clear. Such sentences can be spotted because they included phrases such as: each of; one of; neither of; every one of; not one of; each; every; anybody; everybody; and nobody. In these cases, the subject is actually singular: everybody = every *single* body; nobody = not *one* body; neither of = not *one* of the two. Therefore such sentences use a singular verb:

'All of our grandchildren (plural subject) have done well (plural verb) at school.'
'Each of our grandchildren (singular subject) has done well (singular verb) at school.'
'Anybody (singular) is (singular) eligible for entry.'
'Nobody (singular) wants (singular) to attend.'

However, a plural verb is used when using plural subjects that are separated by the following words: either ... or; neither ... nor; both ... and; all ... but.

'All (plural) but Alice were (plural) present.'
'Either the unions (plural) or the managers (plural) were (plural) to blame.'
'Neither the unions (plural) nor the managers (plural) were (plural) to blame.'
'Both Uncle David and (makes the plural) Aunt Sally have replied (plural) to the invitation.'

Choose the right pronoun

Pronouns are words that stand in place of a noun. They are normally fairly easy to use, unless you are dealing with two people in the same sentence.

'Miss Daisley and I (not 'me') would like to visit your offices.'

'The person who held the keys to the safe was she (not her).'

'We (not 'us') early risers do our most productive work in the mornings.'

The trick is to try the sentence without the other person or the descriptive phrase ('early risers'), or turn the sentence round and see if it sounds right:

'Me would like to visit your offices.'

'Her held the keys to the safe.'

'Us do our most productive work in the mornings.'

The result is, of course, plain nonsense.

Build clear sentences

There are three basic forms of sentence: simple, compound and complex. The simple sentence contains a subject (the cat), a verb (lapped) and an object (the cream). It may also include a preposition if necessary: the cat sat *on* the mat.

Compound sentences have two halves, usually separated by a comma or a connecting word (a conjunction). Compound sentences are in effect two simple sentences joined together:

'The cat sat on the mat. The cat lapped the cream.' (Two simple sentences.)

'The cat sat on the mat and lapped the cream.' (One compound sentence.)

Complex sentences contain a third element, which is usually separated off with punctuation:

'The cat, which was black, sat on the mat and lapped the cream.'

The 'subordinate clause' between the two commas makes this a complex sentence.

SUBJECT-VERB-OBJECT
Whichever form of sentence you are using, try to follow the usual order of words: subject, verb, object. Any other order is unusual in written English, and can make a sentence difficult to read.

By using conjunctions, subordinate clauses, compound, simple and complex sentences, it is possible to vary the length and rhythm of each one, to make your writing more interesting. The following three sentences are monotonous. They all start with the word 'I' and they are all simple sentences. The insertion of a single conjunction makes all the difference:

'I understand that you would like to receive information about our latest range. I am sending you the brochures that we have. I am also enclosing a copy of our price list.'

'I understand that you would like to receive information about our latest range. I am therefore sending you the brochures that we have *along with* our price list.'

Here are some conjunctions that may come in handy when linking short sentences together, and when making sentences flow to form a coherent paragraph. Words that are particularly useful for connecting a paragraph with the preceding one are marked with an asterisk*.

along with
also
although*
and
as a consequence
because of this*
but
by comparison*
consequently
either ... or
finally*
first, second, third
for example
for instance
furthermore
hence
however
in addition*
in conclusion*
in contrast*
in light of this*
in particular
in the first place*
in the same way*
in view of this*
moreover
neither ... nor
nevertheless
not only ... but
on one hand ... on the other
hand
similarly*
so
specifically

subsequently
therefore
to sum up*
to summarize*
too
with regard to*
with this in mind*
yet

Replace pronouns with nouns for clarity

> 'Mrs Morris was angry. She said Mrs Rose was to blame. She had given her her goods, but had failed to include her bill.'

Who did what to whom? There is no way of telling from this explanation. Wherever the subject of a sentence changes, consider using the noun rather than the pronoun to make the situation clear. Any pronoun used should always relate to the last noun given:

> 'Mrs Morris was angry. She said Mrs Rose was to blame. Mrs Rose (new subject) had given Mrs Morris her goods (i.e. they belong to Mrs Morris), but had failed to include the bill.'

Now we know.

Avoid the passive

Passive constructions do not have a subject. Active constructions give both a subject and an object. In the following examples, the first sentence is passive, and the second is active:

> 'Your letter has been passed on to my superior.'
> 'I have passed your letter on to my superior.'
> 'The sales assistant has been reprimanded.'
> 'Mrs Brown has reprimanded the sales assistant.'

> 'The information you require is enclosed.'
> 'I am enclosing the information you require.'

The difference is clear. In the first of each pair, it is not certain who was taking the action. In the second sentence, the subject (the person taking the action) is given. The implication is that this person acted personally on the correspondent's request, and takes responsibility for the action. Active sentences appear more punchy, adding dynamism to your writing.

There is only one instance where a passive construction may be a good idea. This is when it is diplomatic not to name the 'culprit'. A person wishes to reprimand an employee, but does not want to name the informant:

'I have been told' is better than 'Mr James has told me'.
'I notice that the copying department is wasting a large amount of paper ...' could be better worded: 'I notice that a large amount of paper is being wasted.'

The second construction in each pair makes use of the passive to give a feeling of generality: the department may not be deliberately wasting paper, but wastage is occurring. While this cannot literally be the case, the tone of the sentence is less accusatory, and more likely to get results.

Keep the subject close to the verb

This is a useful rule to bear in mind, especially when putting together more complex sentences. It ensures that the reader does not have to wade through several clauses before reaching the point of the sentence:

'The planned improvements, drawn up by management and accepted by the union after a number of meetings at which they finally voted five to one in favour, are designed to increase market share.'

The subject of the sentence appears at the start of the sentence, while the verb – 'are designed to increase' – is left until the end. On a first reading, one has to hold the opening clause 'in suspension' until it is resolved with the verb and the object. The reader may also need to look over the sentence again, in an effort to work out what is being designed, the vote or the improvements. A possible reworking which also removes unnecessary information, is as follows:

'The improvements are designed to increase market share. They were drawn up by management and accepted by the union after a number of meetings.'

The subordinate clause must refer to the subject of the sentence

A subordinate clause is a group of words which adds extra information to a sentence, but which could be removed without changing its essential meaning. A subordinate clause is often marked off from other parts of the sentence with commas, or the word 'which':

'Running to catch the post before the final collection, she saw a man with a wheelbarrow.'

In this sentence, the subordinate clause is placed at the start of the sentence before the comma. The subject of the sentence is 'she', and so, if the clause refers to the subject, she is running to catch the post, and not the man with the wheelbarrow. If the man with the wheelbarrow were running to catch the post (a doughty letter-writer this one), then the sentence must be reworked.

'She saw a man with a wheelbarrow running to catch the post before the last collection.'

Avoid a subordinate clause at the start of a sentence

Many writers agree that the subordinate clause at the start of the sentence is undesirable, and this is certainly the case when writing to young children or foreigners. However, there is no hard and fast rule, except perhaps to make sure that you do not overuse the subordinate clause in this position. If you want to rework a sentence, look for the subject-verb-object word order and change it round accordingly, inserting a suitable conjunction:

'Running to catch the post before the final collection, she saw a man with a wheelbarrow.'
'She was running to catch the post before the final collection *when* she saw a man with a wheelbarrow.'

'Having read your letter several times, I am still unsure of the details of your request.'
'I have read your letter several times, *but* I am still unsure of the details of your request.'

It is easy to spot a subordinate clause at the start of a sentence. It can be identified by the presence of a verb that has 'ing' at the end:

'Hav*ing* read your letter ... '

Building paragraphs

A paragraph is a unit of thought. A single paragraph should contain only the sentences that relate to the subject in question. New subject, new paragraph.

Paragraph focus

If you have difficulty keeping each paragraph of your letter focused on a single idea, try writing a sentence that defines the subject. You may even use that sentence to open the paragraph.

Good early planning and drafting (see pp. 41-49) should enable you to pinpoint the subject of each stage of your letter. When you have drafted the full letter, read through, deleting sentences that stray from the subject of the paragraph. If these sentences relate to different points for which you have no paragraph, you may like to add one.

Connecting paragraphs

Each paragraph should be related to the one before, to help the reader follow your train of thought. There are a number of words and phrases that can be used to connect thoughts in this way. The list on p. 83 gives some ideas.

Developing an idea

When looking over a draft, ensure that each paragraph treats a single idea, and that this idea is expanded enough. Avoid going into too much detail, however. Give just enough detail to be coherent. You may need to add an example to illustrate your thinking, or you may need to show an intermediate stage in your thought process instead of jumping from point A to point C without passing through point B. Always re-read your letter with the reader in mind, and preferably the day after it was drafted. Only then will missing information or irrelevancies become apparent.

Editing checklist

Use the following list to ensure you have not fallen into any of the most common grammar or style traps:

- Look for long sentences: can they be broken into shorter sentences?
- Look for long paragraphs: can they be broken into shorter paragraphs?

- Look for words that you have repeated in the same sentence or paragraph. Can you find alternative words that do the same job?
- Are the verbs in your sentences close to the subject? If not, change the sentence round. (See pp. 85-6.)
- Are your constructions active or passive. Use passive constructions only where they suit your purpose. (See pp. 84-5.)
- Look for clauses with verbs ending in -ing. Is there likely to be any confusion as to the subject of the sentence? (See p. 86.)
- Look for clusters of pronouns. Can you replace them with nouns to improve the reader's understanding? (See p. 84.)
- Have you used several words where a single word would do the job? (See pp. 75-8.)

Bad language and abuse

There may be times when you are so provoked that the air is heavy with expletives. A golden rule for letter-writers is: *never* be abusive in a letter. However angry or upset you may be, and however tempted to convey those sentiments through the mail, don't do it. By all means, if it helps to vent your anger, scrawl down the words you would like to say, but never post them, and don't leave your 'letter' in an envelope on your desk so that some well-meaning person can pick it up and post it for you.

As with most infuriating situations, it is wise to wait a while, until you are calm enough to think reasonably, before committing any communication to the mail. First, words spoken or written in anger are almost always regretted when the passion fades. Second, you may make libellous statements and accusations with the result that you could end up in court (see pp.

151-3). Remember that words written down do not evaporate into the air, there to be quickly forgotten. They stand as a constant reminder of your moment of rage.

Before responding to the object of your anger or frustration, make sure that your views are reasonable, and that you have the facts straight. Choose words that are calm and full of reason. Avoid making direct accusations. Ask your reader to put him- or herself in your position, to try to understand your situation or feelings. Try to find a solution.

A good way to convey your anger and disapproval without resorting to abuse is to omit the usual courtesies built into letter-writing rules. Leave out the salutory 'Dear', and your opening is abrupt – the equivalent of a sharp word. Omit the complimentary close, and you are doing the equivalent of turning your back on the object of your anger, or dismissing them curtly from the room.

The sample letters on pp. 190-92 (**Complaints**) and pp. 201-2 (**Disputes**) give further notes for situations likely to drive you insane.

ADDRESSING AN ENVELOPE

There are two reasons for paying attention to the way you address an envelope. First, a clear address with full details, and positioned correctly on the face of the envelope, enables it to be processed using the postal service's most efficient technology. It is therefore more likely to be delivered at the correct address in the shortest possible time.

Second, the wording on an envelope has the effect of saying 'hello' to the recipient. It gives a first impression, and while you may not be too impressed that the correspondent was a colonel in the armed forces during the Suez Crisis, the Colonel himself may be the kind of person to consider your omission of his title an irritating lack of courtesy and respect. In most circumstances this kind of first impression is not desirable, and following the conventions described in this chapter will help to avoid it.

Postal addresses

In the UK the Royal Mail requests that postal addresses for inland mail contain the following information, with each item placed on a separate line:

- Addressee's title and name.
- Addressee's position in the company (if appropriate).
- Addressee's company name.
- Building number (or name) and street name. Alternatively, this part of the address may be a unit number and the name of an industrial estate or business park.
- Name of locality, village or hamlet.
- Postal town in capital letters.
- County name (or its abbreviation).
- Postcode in capital letters and no punctuation.

It would be possible for the Royal Mail to find a building given only its number and postcode, but to address a letter this way would probably lead to delays, and is not desirable. The post code remains the most important item (apart from the personal details), and it really is a good idea to use it in full. If you do not know the correct postcode, you can find out by calling the Royal Mail's Postcode Enquiry Line: (0345) 111222.

The Royal Mail also asks that you do not punctuate addresses on envelopes, because this makes them difficult for sorting-office machinery to read.

Envelope layout

The recipient's address should be typed or written clearly in the lower half of the front of the envelope, towards the right-hand side. Leave space for stamps or franking slips to be positioned in the top right-hand corner, and remember that the Royal Mail will add a postmark which might obliterate part of a badly-placed address.

If you are handwriting your envelope, indent each successive line of the address as you would inside the letter (see p. 38). If you are typing the envelope, the left-hand edge of each line should line up vertically. Unless you are addressing an unusually large envelope or parcel, it is not necessary to double-space the address. Equally, it is not necessary to add the word 'To:' unless you are addressing a bulky parcel, in which case it would be useful to distinguish between the recipient's and the sender's address.

You may find that an address is too long to fit on to the envelope. In this case, type the postal town and the county on the same line. Alternatively, omit the county and type the postcode on the same line as the postal town, but leave about eight spaces between the two to enable postal workers to find the postcode at a glance.

> **ADDRESSING LETTERS FOR POSTE RESTANTE**
> In many countries, a person's name is written surname
> first. When addressing a letter to a poste restante in a
> foreign country, therefore, it is helpful to underline the
> addressee's surname. Most poste restante facilities sort
> the incoming mail by surname, and so this can help pre-
> vent letters being filed in the wrong place and so being
> overlooked. Many poste restante services abroad charge
> the recipient a fee per item. So, if you can, collect a num-
> ber of letters into a single envelope.

Sender's address

The address of the sender should be written on the outside of
the envelope. Place it on the back flap or on the front of the
envelope in the top left-hand corner. Many companies have
envelopes printed with their address, but if you are writing
letters on personal stationery, it may save you time to have
stickers printed with your name and address for this purpose.
In any case, the most important thing is to avoid any confusion
between the two addresses because of their proximity. This is
particularly important when sending letters overseas.

Parcels should always give both addresses with the words
'To:' and 'From:' in the appropriate places.

It goes without saying that you should always add the correct postage (it is always annoying for a recipient to receive a
letter with a surcharge to pay), and remember to leave space
for the appropriate stickers for any special means of carriage
(registered, recorded delivery, etc.). These will normally be
placed on the left-hand side of the envelope.

> ## ENVELOPES CHECKLIST
>
> **Have you:**
> - **Written the recipient's address correctly and in the right order?**
> - **Included the postcode?**
> - **Added your own address?**
> - **Left space for stamps and other stickers?**
> - **Put everything in the correct position on the envelope?**

Titles and forms of address

The way a person is to be addressed has for centuries been hedged about by the conventions of etiquette within the social hierarchy. While in the past few decades, this hierarchy has become less rigid than it once was, there is still a great deal to be said for knowing how to address a person properly. Even in this day and age, failure to use the correct form of address may be seen by some as ignorance or lack of courtesy. To look at it another way, there are probably a great number of people who would be irritated or even insulted by not being addressed properly, and a very tiny number of people who would object to being given their full title. So if in doubt, err on the side of formality.

People of no rank

Most people have no special title, and so the form of address you would use depends on their sex and, when addressing women, their marital status.

Addressing men

The formal way to address a man is to use his initial(s) and surname, followed by the abbreviation Esq. (for esquire).

However, this form is gradually going out of style (it refers back to the days when knights employed squires), and a plain Mr is becoming more common. Despite this, it is still a good idea to use Esq. for members of the professions. Remember that if a person claims any title at all (e.g. Dr or Professor) you should not use Esq., and never use Esq. and Mr together.

A boy gains the title 'Mr' when he reaches about the age of 16. Some people use the title 'Master' when addressing younger boys, but using the child's Christian and surnames in full will do.

Addressing women

Addressing men is child's play compared to the conventions surrounding the proper way to address a woman. These rules are a leftover from the days when women were considered no more than an appendage to their husbands, and as times have changed so too have the conventions.

Unmarried women and girl children are normally addressed as Miss. But some unmarried women (especially those in business) find any reference to their marital status an unnecessary distinction and prefer to be addressed as Ms. If you do not know the addressee personally, you will be able to find out which title a woman prefers by checking how she signs herself in her own letters, or by calling her, her office or her company's switchboard

Addressing a married woman

A married woman is traditionally known by her husband's name. So Alice Jenkins, the wife of Charles Jenkins, would formally be addressed as Mrs C. Jenkins, or Mrs Charles Jenkins.

However, as more and more married women enter the workforce, and are gradually accepted as individuals in their own right, it is now common to address a married woman using the title 'Mrs', but giving the woman's own Christian name or initial. Therefore, Alice Jenkins the bank manager would be addressed Mrs A. Jenkins or Mrs Alice Jenkins.

Just as some unmarried women wish to avoid continual reference to their marital status in a business context, so married women have also taken to using 'Ms' instead of 'Mrs'. However, it may also be the case that a woman retains her maiden name for business purposes after she has married. In this case in particular, it is important to use Ms. Again, take your lead from the addressee.

Divorced or widowed women

It is usual to address a divorced woman using her own Christain name or initials rather than those of her ex-husband. By contrast, a widow usually continues to be addressed by her husband's Christian name or initials.

Women doctors

If a woman is a doctor, she should be addressed as such, using her Christian name or initials. So, if Alice Jenkins were not a bank manager, but a GP, she would be addressed Dr A. Jenkins, MD. The reasoning goes that the title belongs to her and not to her husband. The same rule applies to the term Professor.

Addressing married couples

In formal letters, married couples are normally addressed using the initials of the husband only: Mr & Mrs C. Jenkins is an example.

At one time it was the convention to address the wife alone when sending personal letters, expecting the husband to have the opportunity to read his wife's correspondence. Nowadays, this is hardly ever done, except when replying to a formal invitation (see p. 221) or thanking a hostess for hospitality (see p. 288).

If there are doctors in the family, use one of the following formulas as appropriate:

- Dr C. & Dr A. Jenkins (if they are both doctors).
- Dr & Mrs C. Jenkins (if the man only is a doctor).
- Mr C. and Dr A. Jenkins (if the woman only is a doctor).

The same rules apply to the term Professor.

MEDICAL CONSULTANTS AND DENTISTS
Once a physician qualifies as a consultant, he or she no longer uses the title 'Dr', but reverts to Mr, Mrs, Miss or Ms. Dentists should also be called by these titles.

Addressing unmarried couples

Of course, there are many couples who are not married, but are living together as if they were, and many have stable families with children without the legal matrimonial ties. In this case, the two individuals should each be addressed by their full names and titles:

> Mr C. Jenkins & Miss A. Hodge *or*
> Mr C. Jenkins & Ms A. Hodge.

DEGREES OF FORMALITY
Obviously, the rules on forms of address are not legally binding, so if you are writing personal and informal letters, you may simply wish to give names and surnames without any title at all. But this would certainly look out of place in a formal or business context unless your addressee is a particularly close colleague of long standing.

ADDRESSING AN ENVELOPE

Members of the armed forces

There are two rules when it comes to addressing members and
ex-members of the armed forces. First, all those below the rank
of commissioned officers and the highest non-commissioned
officers should be addressed by their civilian titles (Mr, Sir,
Lord, etc.). Second, it is usual only to use a person's service
rank when writing to them at their station or on matters concerning service business.

However, some retired members still like to be addressed by
their former service rank, and it would be discourteous to
refuse to do so. As always, take your lead from the addressee.

Addressing royalty, members of the peerage, the clergy and officials

When addressing letters to the more elevated levels of society,
it is wise *always* to use the customary form of address. At these
levels, forms of address relate not only to the correct form of
the addressee's title, but also to special forms for the salutation
and for making references to the recipient in the letter itself.
Furthermore, when writing to the most exalted levels of the
peerage and royalty, there may be related rules about the form
of the subscription.

The following list starts with H.M. The Queen and works its
way through the peerage, clergy and officials, giving details as
appropriate. It lists the form for the envelope, salutation and
subscription, and in some cases the form of any reference to
the addressee within the body of the letter. For example, The
Queen should be referred to as 'Your Majesty' rather than as
'you'.

The forms given for addressing Royalty assume that the
sender is a citizen of the United Kingdom, and therefore a subject. If this is not the case, then the words 'obedient servant'
might be a good replacement for 'faithful subject'.

The Queen

All letters should be addressed to a private secretary unless you are a personal friend or relative, or are already in correspondence with Her Majesty.

Envelope: The Private Secretary to Her Majesty The Queen
Salutation: Dear Sir, Dear Madam or Dear Private Secretary
Subscription: Yours faithfully

However, if you do find yourself in personal correspondence with Her Majesty, the form is as follows:

Envelope: The Queen's Most Excellent Majesty
Salutation: May it please Your Majesty
Subscription: I have the honour to remain, Madam, Your Majesty's faithful subject
Reference: Your Majesty

The Duke of Edinburgh

To a private secretary:
Envelope: The Private Secretary to His Royal Highness (or HRH) The Duke of Edinburgh
Salutation: Dear Sir, Dear Madam or Dear Private Secretary
Subscription: Yours faithfully

To the Duke:

Envelope: HRH The Duke of Edinburgh
Salutation: Your Royal Highness
Subscription: I have the honour to remain, Sir, Your Royal Highness' most dutiful subject
Reference: Your Royal Highness

The Queen Mother

To a private secretary:

Envelope: The Private Secretary to Her Majesty (or HM) The Queen Mother
Salutation and Subscription: As for HM The Queen

To the Queen Mother:
Envelope: Her Majesty (or HM) The Queen Mother
Salutation: May it please your Majesty
Subscription: I have the honour to remain, Madam, Your Majesty's dutiful and obedient subject
Reference: Your Majesty

Prince Charles
To a private secretary:
As for the Duke of Edinburgh, (see p. 99)

To the Prince:
Envelope: His Royal Highness the Prince of Wales
Salutation: Your Royal Highness
Subscription: I have the honour to remain, Sir, your Royal Highness' most dutiful subject
Reference: As salutation

Princess of Wales
Envelope: Her Royal Highness the Princess of Wales
Salutation: Your Royal Highness
Subscription: I have the honour to remain, Madam, your Royal Highness' most dutiful and obedient subject
Reference: As salutation

Prince Andrew
Envelope: His Royal Highness the Duke of York
Salutation: Your Royal Highness
Subscription: I have the honour to remain, Sir, your Royal Highness' most dutiful subject
Reference: As salutation

- This form also applies to other Royal Dukes, such as the Duke of Gloucester.

Duchess of York
Envelope: Her Royal Highness the Duchess of York
Salutation: Your Royal Highness
Subscription: I have the honour to remain, Madam, your Royal Highness' most dutiful and obedient subject
Reference: As salutation
- This form also applies to other Royal Duchesses.

Prince Edward
Envelope: His Royal Highness Prince Edward
Salutation: Your Royal Highness
Subscription: I have the honour to remain, Sir, your Royal Highness' dutiful subject
Reference: As salutation

Princess Anne, The Princess Royal
Envelope: Her Royal Highness the Princess Royal
Salutation: Your Royal Highness
Subscription: I have the honour to remain, Madam, your Royal Highness' dutiful and obedient subject
Reference: As salutation

Princess Margaret
Envelope: Her Royal Highness Princess Margaret
Salutation: Your Royal Highness
Subscription: I have the honour to remain, Madam, your Royal Highness' dutiful and obedient subject
Reference: As salutation

Duke
Envelope: His Grace the Duke of (place)

Salutation: My Lord Duke
Subscription: I have the honour to be your Grace's most obedient servant
Reference: Your Grace

Duchess
Envelope: Her Grace the Duchess of (place)
Salutation: Madam
Subscription: I have the honour to be your Grace's most obedient servant
Reference: Your Grace

Marquess & Marchioness
Envelope: The Marquess/Marchioness of (place)
Salutation: Dear Lord/Lady (place)
Subscription: Yours faithfully/sincerely

Earl & Countess
Envelope: The Earl/Countess of (place)
Salutation: Dear Lord/Lady (place)
Subscription: Yours faithfully/sincerely

Viscount & Viscountess
Envelope: The Viscount/Viscountess (place)
Salutation: Dear Lord/Lady (place)
Subscription: Yours faithfully/sincerely

Baron & Baroness
Envelope: The Lord/Lady (surname)
Salutation: Dear Lord/Lady (surname)
Subscription: Yours faithfully/sincerely

Baronet & wife
Envelope: Sir (Christian name & surname), Bt./Lady (surname)

Salutation: Dear Sir (Christian name)/Lady (surname)
Subscription: Yours faithfully/sincerely

Hereditary peeress
Envelope: The Countess of (place)
Salutation: Dear Lady (place)
Subscription: Yours faithfully/sincerely

Life peer & wife
Envelope: The Lord/Lady (surname)
Salutation: Dear Lord/Lady (surname)
Subscription: Yours faithfully/sincerely

Life peeress
Envelope: Baroness (surname)
Salutation: Dear Lady (surname)
Subscription: Yours faithfully/sincerely

Knight & wife
Envelope: Sir (Christian name & surname)/Lady (surname)
Salutation: Dear Sir (Christian name)/Lady (surname)
Subscription: Yours faithfully/sincerely

Dame
Envelope: Dame (Christian name & surname)
Salutation: Dear Dame (Christian name)
Subscription: Yours faithfully/sincerely

The Pope
Envelope: His Holiness the Pope
Salutation: Your Holiness, Most Holy Father
Subscription: I have the honour to remain your Holiness' most devoted and obedient child (if sender is a Catholic), or 'servant' (if not)
Reference: Your Holiness

Roman Catholic Archbishop
Envelope: His Grace the Archbishop of (place)
Salutation: Dear Archbishop, Your Grace
Subscription: Yours faithfully/sincerely

Roman Catholic Cardinal
Envelope: His Eminence the Cardinal (surname)
Salutation: Your Eminence
Subscription: Yours faithfully/sincerely

Roman Catholic Priest
Envelope: The Reverend (Christian name & surname)
Salutation: Dear Father (surname)
Subscription: Yours faithfully/sincerely

Anglican Archbishop
Envelope: The Most Reverend and Right Honourable the Lord Archbishop of (place)
Salutation: Dear Archbishop
Subscription: Yours faithfully/sincerely

Anglican Bishop
Envelope: The Right Reverend the Lord Bishop of (place)
Salutation: Dear Bishop
Subscription: Yours faithfully/sincerely
- The one exception is the Bishop of London, who is addressed as The Right Reverend and Right Honourable the Lord Bishop of London.

Anglican Vicar
Envelope: The Reverend (Christian name & surname)
Salutation: Dear Mr (surname)
Subscription: Yours faithfully/sincerely

Minister
Envelope: The Reverend (Christian name & surname)
Salutation: Dear Mr/Mrs/Ms (surname)
Subscription: Yours faithfully/sincerely

Chief Rabbi
Envelope: The Chief Rabbi Mr (Christian name & surname)
Salutation: Dear Chief Rabbi
Subscription: Yours faithfully/sincerely

Rabbi
Envelope: Rabbi (Christian name & surname)
Salutation: Dear Rabbi (surname)
Subscription: Yours faithfully/sincerely

Prime Minister
Envelope: The Rt. Hon. (Christian name & surname), MP
Salutation: Dear Prime Minister
Subscription: Yours faithfully/sincerely

Chancellor of the Exchequer
Envelope: The Rt. Hon. (Christian name & surname), PC, MP
Salutation: Dear Chancellor
Subscription: Yours faithfully/sincerely

Secretary of State
Envelope: HM Principal Secretary of State for (Department), or
as for Chancellor of the Exchequer
Salutation: Dear Sir, Dear Madam, Dear Secretary of State
Subscription: Yours faithfully/sincerely

Members of Parliament
Envelope: Christian name (or initials) & surname, MP
Salutation: Dear Mr (or other title as appropriate)
Subscription: Yours faithfully/sincerely

British Ambassador

Envelope: His Excellency HBM's Ambassador & Plenipotentiary
Salutation: My Lord (and other according to rank)
Reference: Your Excellency
Subscription: Yours faithfully/sincerely

Lord Mayor/Lady Mayor

Envelope: The Right Worshipful the Lord (Lady) Mayor
Salutation: My Lord (Lady) Mayor
Subscription: Yours faithfully/sincerely

- For the cities of York, Cardiff, Dublin and Belfast, the Mayor is addressed as The Rt. Hon. the Lord (Lady) Mayor of (place)

Lady Mayoress

Envelope: The Lady Mayoress of (place)
Salutation: My Lady Mayoress
Subscription: Yours faithfully/sincerely

- The difference between the Lady Mayor and the Lady Mayoress is that the Lady Mayor is Mayor in her own right, whereas the Lady Mayoress is in office by virtue of being the wife of the Mayor.

Councillor

Envelope: Councillor Mr/Mrs (surname)
Salutation: Dear Councillor
Subscription: Yours faithfully/sincerely

Honours and decorations

Personal honours are taken by people who have earned an educational qualification, belong to a professional body, or hold office. They are normally indicated in a person's title by the addition of letters after the name. A number of these honours also bring with them a title. Doctor and Professor are two examples of this.

It may seem like a waste of time to discover what honours a correspondent may hold, and indeed, some people fail to list their honours at all. However, a look at a person's stationery or signature should indicate whether your addressee finds these things important. If it is obvious that they do, then you should do likewise.

If a person has gained more than one honour in a particular field (perhaps she gained a BA followed by an MA and then a Doctorate), it is usual to list only the highest of these honours. However, academic honours in different fields of study should be listed separately in order of prestige, starting with the lowest.

MDs AND PhDs

All those who have received a doctorate are entitled to call themselves Doctor. A physician will list the letters 'MD' after the name. Doctors of Philosophy also call themselves 'Dr', but list the letters D Phil or PhD after the name.

Decorations are similar sets of initials indicating that a person has received a medal or title.

The following is a list of the honours and decorations possible in the UK. They are given in order of precedence, so that a baronet with a Masters degree who has also been awarded the Order of the British Empire would list his honours in the following order: Bt, OBE, MA.

- Esq. (Esquire) and Bt (Baronet).
- Decorations and orders (e.g. VC, OBE, CBE, GC).
- The following appointments:
    Privy Councillor (PC)
    Aide de Camp to HM the Queen (ADC)
    Honorary Physician to HM the Queen (QHP)

    Honorary Surgeon to HM the Queen (QHS)
    Honorary Dental Surgeon to HM the Queen (QHDS)
    Honorary Nursing Sister to HM the Queen (QHNS)
    Honorary Chaplain to HM the Queen (QHC).

- Educational degrees (e.g. BA, BSc, MA, MSc, MBA, PhD, DPhil).
- Medical qualifications and religious orders.
- Memberships and Fellowships of learned societies and professional bodies (e.g. FRGS, FRCS, FRCP).
- The following appointments:
    Queen's Council (QC)
    Justice of the Peace (JP)
    Deputy Lieutenant (DL)
    Member of Parliament (MP).
- Membership of the armed forces.

Multiple titles

It is sometimes the case that an individual holds more than one title. An army general, for example, may also be a baronet. As a rule of thumb, earned titles (professorships, doctorates, service ranks, etc.) come before inherited titles. Thus George Rayner, who is an army general and a baronet, should properly be called General Sir George. However, many people with multiple titles rarely use them all. Once again, do as they do.

NOTES FOR OFFICE WORKERS

People who are involved in businesses, large or small, have to deal with large quantities of correspondence every day. Efficiency of communication is at the top of the priority list for any business, and so knowing how to draft a short, unambiguous letter is vital to any person working in an office. Previous chapters have dealt with these skills.

Next on the list of priorities comes effectiveness in handling each letter as it comes in and each letter as it goes out, from the time it is conceived by the writer, to the moment it is dropped into the post and a copy filed. Inefficiency in these areas of office life soon become clear to outside colleagues and customers: letters are mislaid, file copies cannot be found, the enclosures, and even letters, are placed in the wrong envelopes for despatch. To prevent this kind of chaos, the letter-production line should be streamlined and carefully monitored.

This chapter follows an outgoing letter from its early life on a dictating machine, to despatch, and then looks at the journey of an incoming letter from mail room to desk.

Dictating letters

Although the more widespread access of executives to word-processing equipment has meant that in some companies, the letter-writing function has been decentralized, many companies still find that dividing the function between two or more people remains the most cost-efficient method of working. This leaves executives free to spend more time in action and less in correspondence, and the more routine roles of keying and despatch are delegated to more specialized personnel. The dictating of letters, either to a secretary or on to a dictating machine, is still a common task.

Dictating is a process of turning the spoken word into written language. Units of speech are very often much longer than written sentences, but we are able to convey a sense of meaning without grammar by using inflections and gestures. The first skill to learn is to speak as you would write: in grammatically constructed sentences.

In the early stages, dictation is made very much easier by jotting down notes or even a full draft of the letter before beginning to dictate. Even a simple list of key words will help you to get the points in the right order. If the letter is more complicated than usual, you may ask the typist to give you a transcription, rather than a fully laid-out letter, so that you can edit it further.

You will also need to give the typist enough information to address the letter correctly and include necessary enclosures:

- Full name and address of recipient.
- Date or even a copy of the previous letter from that correspondent.
- Reference number for any standard letter form you may be using (see p. 29).
- Reference number for this letter, when it is your responsibility to allocate one.
- List of enclosures.
- Names of those people to receive copies of your letter.
- Type of postage/despatch if not ordinary first class.
- Indication of the size/type of stationery to be used, especially if you are in the habit of mixing business with personal correspondence. (See pp. 8-18.)

Dictate in short sentences, even if they seem too short. Speak slowly. Spell out words and names that the transcriber is not likely to be familiar with.

Ensure that the tapes you use are labelled: you might decide on a system whereby there is one tape for every day of the week, so that your dictation can be transcribed in date order. Whatever system you decide on, make sure that you and your typist are careful to implement it. Nothing is more infuriating than losing a whole morning's dictation on a tape that has sprouted legs and walked away.

House style

Most offices have a house style for laying out and punctuating letters. A newcomer will be able to find out what the preferred style is (fully-blocked, semi-blocked, etc.) by looking back in the files. See **Layout and Component Parts** (pp. 26-7) for details of the styles most commonly used.

Form letters

Compiling a set of form letters will save time when you need to respond to large numbers of letters that require s imilar answers. It may be useful to make a file of form letters, giving each a reference number, so that the typist can find the form you are specifying and retype it, making the amendments you require. This system is especially effective if you are using a word processor with the letters stored on disk.

For large numbers of form letters, the mailmerge facility included in the majority of word-processor packages can make life easy. See p. 206.

If you are using a typewriter and photocopier to produce form letters, keep in mind the following points:

- Make a good number of photocopies, using a high-quality photocopier. If your office copier is not up to scratch, you may need to have the photocopying carried out by a bureau.

- Keep the original in a safe place – somewhere it cannot be rumpled and dog-eared.
- If you need to make a further batch of copies, use the original and not a photocopy – the results from a photocopy will be poor.
- When making amendments using a typewriter, make sure that the new words are typed using either exactly the same typeface, or one that is completely different.

Copies for the file

It is always advisable to keep a 'hard copy' of every letter that leaves the office, filed in a suitable place (see pp. 118-19). People often have to refer to previous correspondence, and in some cases, letters may be used as important evidence in legal disputes. While keeping copies on electronic files may save space and paper, there is always the fear that disks will be corrupted or wiped, and the information on them lost.

It is usual to make file copies using paper that is lighter than the company stationery (see p. 15 for weights), and has no letterhead printed on it. This saves expensive printed stationery and means that paper files contain more sheets for less bulk.

When sending a fax or an electronic mail (E-mail) transmission, it is still necessary to make a file copy. Although in the case of a fax, the office receives the original back when the fax transmission is complete, this should be sent on to the recipient by post. This enables the recipient to file a 'hard copy' along with ordinary letters and acts as a double check that the communication has been received.

With E-mail, no hard copy is produced for transmission, because the information is sent direct from the screen. However, that extra couple of minutes spent making a hard copy could prevent chaos if a computer disk is destroyed.

Copies to third parties

If you are sending copies to people other than the addressee, it is usual to indicate this fact after the signatory (see p. 36), with the abbreviation 'cc', followed by the names of the people receiving copies.

If you wish to send a copy of the letter to someone other than the recipient, but without their knowledge, make a note of this fact on the file copy only. The abbreviation 'bc' (blind copy) after the signatory is usual. Some people also highlight the name of the recipient of the copy with a marker.

CORRECTING COPIES

If you are using a typewriter and carbon paper, remember to make any corrections to the bottom copy as well as the top copy.

Stationery

Many companies make do with bad printing, poor typing and shabby envelopes. A letter – any letter – is an advertisement that communicates to the recipient information about the sender's proficiency, professionalism and prosperity. Every business should therefore invest in the best possible company stationery, with a well-designed (if not professionally-produced) letterhead or logo.

It may be acceptable to re-use old envelopes for in-company messages or letters to suppliers of long-standing, but always find the best stationery and envelopes for customers, the bank manager, and other correspondents whose opinion of you is so vital.

See pp. 8-16 for further details on stationery.

USE OF BUSINESS STATIONERY

Never use business stationery unless you are writing in your business capacity. Company letterhead should never be used for business that does not relate to your position in the company; it will confuse the recipient and may be considered an abuse of your position. This is not only because you are appropriating company property for your private purposes, but because everything you write on company stationery carries the authority of your standing within the company and your company's standing in the business world.

Checking outgoing mail

Before mail is released for despatch, it should be checked. This normally falls to the person who is signing the letters, but a glance by the person who puts the letter into the envelope may pick up errors. Make the following checks:

- Does the inside address correspond in all details to the address typed on the envelope?
- Does the letter contain any spelling errors?
- Does the letter have the correct date on it?
- Has the letter been signed, either by the sender or *per procurationem* (see p. 35)?
- If the letter is marked personal or confidential, has the envelope been marked in the same way?
- Are the continuation sheets included, and are they in the correct order?
- Does the envelope contain all enclosures?
- Have all the necessary copies been made?

Routine for despatch

Many offices have a strict routine for despatching letters and parcels, and this may include recording the details of every single letter in a despatch book.

A despatch book is a precise record of correspondence, and acts as a record of stamps used. It may include the following details:

- Date.
- Balance of stamps brought forward from the previous day.
- Name of addressee and location.
- Method of posting.
- Amount of postage.
- Balance of stamps.
- New stamp supplies bought that day.

Outgoing mail should be divided into separate bundles depending on the type of despatch required: first class, second class, special delivery, air mail, etc. Letters should be 'faced', that is, turned round so that they all face the same way, and the bundles should be secured with a rubber band.

Make a final check that all documentation for special mail (recorded delivery, registered, etc.) has been completed correctly and is included.

Incoming mail

When dealing with mail entering the business, the key is speed. Staff who open the mail should do so quickly to ensure that it reaches the correct person as early as possible in the day. This means that a response can be sent by return of post if necessary, and that urgent matters can be dealt with promptly.

Date stamping

It is a very good idea to stamp every letter with the date of its arrival. There are several instances where this may be useful. Staff members who are absent then have a record of the arrival of letters and can deal with the backlog in date order. In some businesses, inquiries are dealt with in date order, and so date-stamping is doubly important. Letters that have been delayed in the post can be identified, and the reason for apparent inaction can be relayed to the sender.

Letters that are marked 'Private', 'Personal' or 'Confidential', and therefore may not be opened immediately on arrival can be stamped with the date on the front of the envelope.

INCOMING MAIL CHECKLIST

- When the mail arrives, deal with it immediately so that it arrives with the right person as soon as possible.
- Open each letter and package and date-stamp them. Letters marked 'personal', 'private', or 'confidential' should be opened only by the designated person (see p. 30), but can be stamped on the envelope.
- Scan each letter for details of enclosures, and check that they are there. If not, make a note at the foot of the letter. Staple the enclosures to the letter if necessary to stop them going astray.
- If the letter includes remittances, check that they tally with the figure mentioned in the remittance advice (see p. 280) or letter.
- Make a note of remittances in a book if this is company policy.
- Check the letter for the sender's address, which may be written only on the envelope. If this is the case, staple the envelope to the letter.
- Sort the mail according to the addressee. You may have to make a decision if the letter gives only a vague idea.

Some secretaries sort mail for their managers into a certain order. This helps the manager deal with the most important items first.

- Confidential and personal letters at the top.
- Letters marked urgent.
- Routine mail.
- Circulars, magazines and newspapers on the bottom.

Signature on delivery

Many items need to be signed for when they are delivered: registered post, recorded delivery, couriered letters, etc. Ideally, it is best to detail only one person to be responsible for accepting such deliveries and passing them on to the correct person. It may even be worthwhile keeping a log of incoming 'special' deliveries of this kind. This avoids wasted time when a delivery goes astray, and the person who signed for it cannot be found. Most communications sent in this manner are important and possibly vital, so a trustworthy person should be on hand to ensure the process runs smoothly.

Acknowledgments

Some companies find themselves with a backlog of letters to answer: when dealing with large numbers of job applicants, for example, or when advertising an enquiry service. No letter should go unanswered for more than a few days – that is simply bad manners, and makes the correspondent suspect that you do not care.

The answer is the routine despatch of acknowledgments – short notes that confirm the arrival of the letter/application/enquiry and to assure the correspondent that they will receive a full response shortly. (See pp. 160-62.)

To save time, acknowledgments can be typed or printed on to postcards, and the name added by hand or typed.

NOTES FOR OFFICE WORKERS

Filing letters

The information given in letters is the life-blood of a success-ful business. Correspondence is a written record of a relation-ship with a client or supplier, and a source of names and addresses for mailing lists. It is vitally important, therefore, that letters are kept and filed in a suitable system, so that any-one can find the information they are looking for and do so quickly.

Simplicity is the watchword when setting up a filing system. Common sense should enable anyone to put documents in the right place and to look in the right place when seeking a par-ticular file. Many systems are set up by one person with so many quirks known only to them, that any other person trying to use the system has no hope of doing so quickly.

Try arranging files under one of the following systems:

- Companies/customers by geographical area (towns, counties, countries) with the individual files sorted alphabetically.
- Companies/customers sorted alphabetically.
- Using a reference number system that identifies the customer and the date or other information.
- Using a reference number that identifies the position of the paper file, and the position of the cabinet among rows of others.

The system that works best for your company will depend on the structure of your business and the type of information you want to store apart from correspondence. Some offices may even require two separate filing systems, but more than two will be difficult to implement and time-consuming to operate. Whichever system is chosen, make sure that it is con-sistent, and that it is maintained properly, especially when folders and cabinets are full and need to be emptied into archive space.

Avoid marking files 'miscellaneous'. This is the sign of a poorly thought-out system. A 'miscellaneous' file is a file of unfiled files, and so not a file at all. It might just as well be the waste-paper basket.

FILING FOR PROTECTION

Filing serves two purposes: it enables access to information; and it protects that information from damage or loss. Important documents and letters such as legal letters should be protected in a fire-proof safe. Confidential documents should be kept under lock and key, away from prying eyes.

Indexing the system

Filing systems should be accessible to everyone, and not just the person who uses it every day. An index to the system, attached to the side of a cabinet or circulated periodically to staff, will enable people to find letters fast and file (or re-file) items quickly. The index could give the file name or the reference number and the name, depending on the system being operated.

Order within files

Inside paper files, correspondence is most often filed in reverse chronological order, that is with the most recent letter at the front. Take the date of despatch or the date of arrival as the guide for this, but whichever date you decide on, be consistent.

If you need to consult a particular letter in a file, it is better to photocopy the letter you require and return the file intact, than to remove the letter itself. This ensures that file copies do not go astray, and that files are available for consultation by others for as much of the time as possible.

Another check is to ask people removing files from the cabinet to note down the details in a register, giving their name and department and the time they expect to be finished with the file.

Using abbreviations for efficiency

The business world has a special language which includes all sorts of abbreviations that enable people to communicate quickly.

Abbreviations are words that have been shortened. When the abbreviation does not include the last letter of the original word, it should be followed by a full stop. A contraction, on the other hand, includes the last letter of the original word, and therefore does not need a full stop. Abbreviations of the names of companies or institutions are often made by listing just the initials of the original words (BBC, IBM, ICI). Sometimes these initials are written with full stops between each letter, and sometimes not. If in doubt, find out what the company or institution itself prefers to do on its own letterhead (modern usage is now tending towards leaving the full stops out altogether). Acronyms are strings of initials that make up a 'word' (UNICEF, UNESCO, NATO). Acronyms never have full stops.

The following list contains many of the abbreviations you may come across when dealing with forms of address or other parts of business correspondence.

AA	Alcoholics Anonymous, Automobile Association
AACCA	Associate of the Association of Certified and Corporate Accountants
a/c	account
AC	Assistant Commissioner
ACA	Associate of the Institute of Chartered Accountants

ACAS	The Advisory, Conciliation and Arbitration Service
ACII	Associate of the Chartered Insurance Institute
ACIS	Associate of the Chartered Institute of Secretaries
ack.	acknowledge
ACM	Air Chief-Marshal
AD	anno Domini (in the year of our Lord, after Christ)
ADC	Aide-de-Camp
add.	addendum
ad lib.	*ad libitum* (at leisure)
ADP	automatic data processing
ad val.	ad valorem (according to the value)
AERE	Atomic Energy Research Establishment
AFA	Associate of the Faculty of Actuaries
AFAS	Associate of the Faculty of Architects and Surveyors
AFC	Air Force Cross
AFM	Air Force Medal
AFS	Associate of the Faculty of Secretaries
AG	*Aktiengesellschaft* (German public company)
AGM	annual general meeting
AH	*anno Hegirae* (the Muslim era, similar to the Christian AD)
AIC	Associate of the Institute of Chemistry
AICE	Associate of the Institute of Civil Engineers
AIL	Associate of the Institute of Linguists
AIMechE	Associate of the Institution of Mechanical Engineers
AIMinE	Associate of the Institution of Mining Engineers
AISA	Associate of the Incorporated Secretaries' Association

a.k.a. *or* AKA	also known as
ALA	Associate of the Library Association
a.m. *or* am	ante meridiem (before noon)
AMC	Association of Municipal Corporations
AMICE	Associate Member of the Institution of Civil Engineers
AMIChemE	Associate Member of the Institute of Chemical Engineers
AMIEE	Associate Member of the Institution of Electrical Engineers
AMIMechE	Associate Member of the Institution of Mechanical Engineers
AMIMinE	Associate Member of the Institution of Mining Engineers
AMIRE	Associate Member of the Institution of Radio Engineers
AMIStructE	Associate Member of the Institution of Structural Engineers
AOB	any other business
appx	appendix
APS	Associate of the Pharmaceutical Society
ARA	Associate of the Royal Academy
ARAD	Associate of the Royal Academy of Dancing
ARAeS	Associate of the Royal Aeronautical Society
ARAM	Associate of the Royal Academy of Music
ARCM	Associate of the Royal College of Music
ARCO	Associate of the Royal College of Organists
ARCS	Associate of the Royal College of Science
ARIBA	Associate of the Royal Institute of British Architects
ARSA	Associate of the Royal Scottish Academy, Associate of the Royal Society of Arts
ARWS	Associate of the Royal Society of Painters in Water Colours

ASA	Advertising Standards Authority
ASAA	Associate of the Society of Incorporated Accountants and Auditors
ASE	Amalgamated Society of Engineers
ASLEF	Amalgamated Society of Locomotive Engineers and Firemen
assoc.	association/associate(d)
av.	average
Ave	avenue
AVM	Air Vice-Marshal
BA	Bachelor of Arts
BAA	British Airports Authority
BAgr(ic)	Bachelor of Agriculture
BBC	British Broadcasting Corporation
BC	before Christ
bc	blind copy
BCh	Bachelor of Surgery
BChD	Bachelor of Dental Surgery
BCL	Bachelor of Civil Law
BComm	Bachelor of Commerce
BD	Bachelor of Divinity
BDS	Bachelor of Dental Surgery
b.e. or BE	bill of exchange
BEd	Bachelor of Education
BEM	British Empire Medal
BEng	Bachelor of Engineering
BIM	British Institute of Management
bk	bank, book
bkcy	bankruptcy
bkpt	bankrupt
B/L, b/l or b.l.	bill of lading
BL	Bachelor of Law/Letters, British Legion
BLitt	Bachelor of Letters
BM	Bachelor of Medicine, British Museum,

	Brigade-Major
BMA	British Medical Association
BMus	Bachelor of Music
BOTB	British Overseas Trade Board
BPhil	Bachelor of Philosophy
BR	British Rail
BRCS	British Red Cross Society
B/S or b/s	bill of sale
BS	British Standard, Bachelor of Surgery
bs	balance sheet, bill of sale
BSc	Bachelor of Science
BSI	British Standards Institution
BT	British Telecom
Bt or Bart	Baronet
BTG	British Technology Group
c.	circa (roughly this date)
C	Celsius
CA	Chartered Accountant, Consumers' Association
CAB	Citizens' Advice Bureau
CACM	Central American Common Market
CADCAM	computer-aided design, computer-aided manufacture
CADMAT	computer-aided design, manufacture and test
C & D	collection and delivery
C & F	cost and freight
Cantab.	from Cambridge University
CAP	Common Agricultural Policy
cap.	capital
CARICOM	Caribbean Community and Common Market
CB	cash book
CB	Commander of the Order of the Bath
CBE	Commander of the Order of the British Empire
CBI	Confederation of British Industry
CC	County Council

cc	copies
CCT	Common Customs Tariff
CCTV	closed-circuit television
CEO	chief executive officer
cf.	*confer* (compare)
CGM	Conspicuous Gallantry Medal
CGT	capital gains tax
CH	Companion of Honour
ChB	Bachelor of Surgery
ChM	Master of Surgery
chq	cheque
CIE	Companion of the Order of the Indian Empire
c.i.f. *or* CIF	cost, insurance and freight
CIGS	Chief of the Imperial General Staff
CIM	computer-integrated manufacture
C-in-C	Commander-in-Chief
Cllr	Councillor
CM	Master of Surgery, Certificated Master, Corresponding Member
cm	centimetre
CMG	Commander of the Order of St Michael and St George
C/N	consignment note, cover note, credit note
c/o	care of, carried over, cash order
Co *or* Co.	company, county
CO	commanding officer
COI	Central Office of Information
COM	computer output on microfilm
comm.	commission, committee
Comr	Commissioner
Cons.	Conservative, Consul
contd *or* cont'd	continued
COREPER	Committee of Permanent Representatives
CPS	Keeper of the Privy Seal

CR	Keeper of the Rolls
CSI	Companion of the Order of the Star of India
CSM	company sergeant-major
CV	curriculum vitae
CVO	Commander of the Royal Victorian Order
Cx	contrast
DA	Diploma of Art, District Attorney
DBE	Dame of the Order of the British Empire
DCL	Doctor of Civil Law
DCM	Distinguished Conduct Medal
DCMG	Dame Commander of the Order of St Michael and St George
DCVO	Dame Commander of the Royal Victorian Order
DD	Doctor of Divinity
DDS	Doctor of Dental Surgery
DF	Defender of the Faith
DFC	Distinguished Flying Cross
DFM	Distinguished Flying Medal
DG	by the grace of God, thanks be to God
DL	Deputy Lieutenant
DLitt	Doctor of Letters
DM	Deutschmark
DMus	Doctor of Music
do	ditto, the same as before
DOMS	Diploma in Ophthalmic Medicine and Surgery
dos	disk operating system
DP	data processing
DPH	Diploma of Public Health
DPhil	Doctor of Philosophy
DQMG	Deputy Quartermaster-General
Dr	doctor
DSC	Distinguished Service Cross
DSc	Doctor of Science

DSM	Distinguished Service Medal
DSO	Distinguished Service Order
DTh	Doctor of Theology
DTP	desktop publishing
E & OE	errors and ommissions excepted
EC	European Community
ECOWAS	Economic Community of West African States
ECS	*échantillons commerciaux* (commercial samples)
ECU	European currency units
EDP	electronic data processing
EE	Envoy Extraordinary
EEC	European Economic Community
EFTA	European Free Trade Association
EGM	extraordinary general meeting
enc. *or* enc(s)	enclosed, enclosures
ER	Elizabeth Regina (Queen Elizabeth II)
ERDF	European Regional Development Fund
ERM	European Exchange Rate Mechanism
ESOPS	employee share ownership plan
Esq	Esquire
F	fahrenheit
fac.	facsimile
FACCA	Fellow of the Association of Certified and Corporate Accountants
FAI	Fellow of the Chartered Auctioneers' and Estate Agents' Institute
FAS	Fellow of the Antiquarian Society, Fellow of the Anthropological Society
fax	facsimile
FBA	Fellow of the British Academy, Fellow of the British Association
FBOA	Fellow of the British Optical Association
FCA	Fellow of the Institute of Chartered Accountants

FCP	Fellow of the College of Preceptors
FEIS	Fellow of the Educational Institute of Scotland
ff	following
FFA	Fellow of the Faculty of Actuaries
ffy	faithfully
FGS	Fellow of the Geological Society
FIA	Fellow of the Institute of Actuaries
FIAC	Fellow of the Institute of Company Accountants
FIAS	Fellow of the Incorporated Association of Architects and Surveyors
FIJ	Fellow of the Institute of Journalists
FIL	Fellow of the Institute of Linguists
FIPM	Fellow of the Institute of Personnel Management
FISA	Fellow of the Incorporated Secretaries' Association
FISE	Fellow of the Institution of Sanitary Engineers
FLA	Fellow of the Library Association
Flt-Lt	Flight-Lieutenant
FM	Field-Marshal
FPS	Fellow of the Pharmaceutical Society
fr.	franc
FRAM	Fellow of the Royal Academy of Music
FRAS	Fellow of the Royal Astronomical Society, Fellow of the Royal Asiatic Society
FRBS	Fellow of the Royal Society of British Sculptors
FRCM	Fellow of the Royal College of Music
FRCO	Fellow of the Royal College of Organists
FRCP	Fellow of the Royal College of Physicians
FRCS	Fellow of the Royal College of Surgeons
FRCVS	Fellow of the Royal College of Veterinary Surgeons
FRGS	Fellow of the Royal Geographical Society

FRHist-Soc	Fellow of the Royal Historical Society
FRHS	Fellow of the Royal Horticultural Society
FRIBA	Fellow of the Royal Institute of British Architects
FRIC	Fellow of the Royal Institute of Chemistry
FRICS	Fellow of the Royal Institution of Chartered Surveyors
FRMets	Fellow of the Royal Meteorological Society
FRPS	Fellow of the Royal Faculty of Physicians and Surgeons
FRS	Fellow of the Royal Society
FRSA	Fellow of the Royal Society of Arts
FRSE	Fellow of the Royal Society of Edinburgh
FRSGS	Fellow of the Royal Scottish Geographical Society
FRSL	Fellow of the Royal Society of Literature
FRSSA	Fellow of the Royal Scottish Society of Arts
FSA	Fellow of the Royal Society of Antiquaries
FSAA	Fellow of the Society of Incorporated Accountants and Auditors
FSE	Fellow of the Society of Engineers
FSS	Fellow of the Royal Statistical Society
FZS	Fellow of the Zoological Society of London
GATT	General Agreement on Tariffs and Trade
GBE	Grand Cross of the Order of the British Empire
GC	George Cross
GCB	Knight Grand Cross of the Order of the Bath
GCIE	Knight Grand Commander of the Order of the Indian Empire
GCMG	Knight Grand Cross of the Order of St Michael and St George
GCSI	Knight Grand Commander of the Order of the Star of India
GCVO	Grand Cross of the Royal Victorian Order

GM	George Medal
GmbH	*Gesellschaft mit beschrankter Haftung* (German limited company)
GP	general practitioner
HBM	His/Her Britannic Majesty
HC	House of Commons
HE	His/Her Excellency/Eminence
HH	His/Her Highness, His Holiness
HIH	His/Her Imperial Highness
HL	House of Lords
HM	His/Her Majesty
HMC	Her Majesty's Customs
HMS	His/Her Majesty's Service, Her/His Majesty's Ship
HMSO	His/Her Majesty's Stationery Office
Hon. Sec.	Honorary Secretary
Hon.	the Honourable
HRH	His/Her Royal Highness
HSH	His/Her Serene Highness
ICA	Institute of Chartered Accountants
ILO	International Labour Organization
IMF	International Monetary Fund
Inc., Incorp	incorporated
incl.	including
infm. *or* info	information
inst	of this month
Inst.	Institute
InstCE	Institution of Civil Engineers
InstEE	Institution of Electrical Engineers
IT	information technology
ital.	italic
JCD	Doctor of Civil Law, Doctor of Canon Law
JD	Doctor of Laws
JP	Justice of the Peace

JUD	Doctor of Canon and Civil Law
KB	Knight Bachelor, Knight of the Bath
KBE	Knight Commander of the Order of the British Empire
KCB	Knight Commander of the Order of the Bath
KCIE	Knight Commander of the Order of the Indian Empire
KCMG	Knight Commander of the Order of St Michael and St George
KCSI	Knight Commander of the Order of the Star of India
KCVO	Knight Commander of the Royal Victorian Order
KG	Knight of the Garter
KP	Knight of St Patrick
KT	Knight of the Order of the Thistle
Kt	Knight
LAFTA	Latin American Free Trade Association
LCP	Licentiate of the College of Preceptors
LDS	Licentiate of Dental Surgery
LFAS	Licentiate of the Faculty of Architects and Surveyors
LFPS	Licentiate of the Faculty of Physicians and Surgeons
LittD	Doctor of Letters
LL.B.	Bachelor of Laws
LL.M.	Master of Laws
LLCM	Licentiate of the London College of Music
LP	Letters Patent
LRAM	Licentiate of the Royal Academy of Music
LRCM	Licentiate of the Royal College of Music
LRCP	Licentiate of the Royal College of Physicians
LRCS	Licentiate of the Royal College of Surgeons
LRCVS	Licentiate of the Royal College of Veterinary

	Surgeons
LRIBA	Licentiate of the Royal Institute of British Architects
LSA	Licentiate of the Society of Apothecaries
Lt	Lieutenant
Lt-Cdr	Lieutenant-Commander
Lt-Col	Lieutenant-Colonel
Lt-Gen	Lieutenant-General
Ltd	Limited
M	Mr (French)
MA	Master of Arts
MB	Bachelor of Medicine
MBA	Master of Business Administration
MBE	Member of the Order of the British Empire
MC	Military Cross
MCh	Master of Surgery
MComm	Master of Commerce
MCPS	Member of the Royal College of Physicians and Surgeons
MD	Doctor of Medicine, managing director
MEd	Master of Education
MEP	Member of the European Parliament
Mgr	Monsignor
mgr	manager
MICE	Member of the Institution of Civil Engineers
MIEE	Member of the Institution of Electrical Engineers
MIMecgE	Member of the Institution of Mechanical Engineers
Mlle	Miss (French)
MM	Messrs (French), Military Medal
Mme	Mrs (French)
MO	Medical Officer
MOH	Medical Officer of Health

MP	Member of Parliament
MRSA	Member of the Royal Society of Arts
MS	Master of Surgery
MSc	Master of Science
mtg	meeting
MusB	Bachelor of Music
MusD	Doctor of Music
MVO	Member of the Royal Victoran Order
NALGO	National and Local Government Officers' Association
NATO	North Atlantic Treaty Organization
NCO	Non-Commissioned Officer
NCR	no carbon required
NFBTO	National Federation of Building Trades Operatives
NFU	National Farmers' Union
NGO	non-governmental organization
NI	National Insurance
NIC	newly industrialized country
NIS	not in stock
NL	no liability (Australian limited company)
np	new paragraph
NP	Notary Public
npo	non-profit making organization
NV	*Naamloze Venootschap* (Dutch plc)
ob.	obit (deceased)
OBE	Officer of the Order of the British Empire
OECD	Organization for Economic Co-operation and Development
OFT	Office of Fair Trading
OGM	ordinary general meeting
OHMS	On Her Majesty's Service
OHP	overhead projector
OM	Order of Merit

oos	out of stock
OPEC	Organization of Petroleum Exporting Countries
Oxon	from Oxford University
P & L	profit and loss
p & p	postage and packing
para	paragraph
PAYE	pay as you earn
PC	personal computer, Privy Councillor
p/d	post dated
PhD	Doctor of Philosophy
plc *or* PLC	public limited company
p.m. *or* pm	post meridiem (after noon)
PM	Prime Minister, Provost Marshal
PMG	Paymaster General
PO	Petty Officer, Pilot Officer, postal order
pp	*post procurationem* (for and on behalf of)
PPI	printed postage impression
pps	additional postscript
pqe	post-qualification experience
Pres.	president
Prof.	professor
ps	postscript
Pta	peseta
Pte	Private (army)
QB	Queen's Bench
QC	Queen's Counsel
QHC	Queen's Honorary Chaplain
QHDS	Queen's Honorary Dental Surgeon
QHNS	Queen's Honorary Nursing Sister
QHP	Queen's Honorary Physician
QHS	Queen's Honorary Surgeon
quango	quasi-autonomous non-governmental organization
qy	query
R & D	research and development

RA	Royal Academician, Royal Artillery
RADA	Royal Academy of Dramatic Art
RADC	Royal Army Dental Corps
RAEC	Royal Army Educational Corps
RAF	Royal Air Force
RAM	random-access memory, Royal Academy of Music
RAMC	Royal Army Medical Corps
RAOC	Royal Army Ordnance Corps
RAPC	Royal Army Pay Corps
RAVC	Royal Army Veterinary Corps
RCA	Royal College of Art
rcd	received
RCM	Royal College of Music
RCP	Royal College of Preceptors, Royal College of Physicians
RCS	Royal College of Surgeons
RCVS	Royal College of Veterinary Surgeons
RE	Royal Engineers
re	with reference to
Rear-Adm	Rear-Admiral
ref.	refer to
Reg. Prof.	Regius Professor
REME	Royal Electrical and Mechanical Engineers
retd	retired
RGS	Royal Geographical Society
RHistSoc	Royal Historical Society
RHS	Royal Horticultural Society
RIBA	Royal Institute of British Architects
RICS	Royal Institution of Chartered Surveyors
RIPH	Royal Institute of Public Health
RM	Royal Marines
RMP	Royal Military Police
RN	Royal Navy

RNR	Royal Naval Reserve
RNVR	Royal Naval Volunteer Reserve
ROM	read-only memory
RR	Right Reverend
RSA	Royal Scottish Academician, Royal Society of Arts, Royal Society of Antiquaries
RSAM	Royal Scottish Academy of Music
RSM	Regimental Sergeant-Major, Royal Society of Medicine
RSVP	*répondez s'il vous plaît* (please reply)
Rt Hon.	Right Honourable
Rt Revd	Right Reverend
RWS	Royal Society of Painters in Water Colours
SA	*société anonyme* (public limited company)
sae	stamped addressed envelope
SAYE	save as you earn
ScB	Bachelor of Science
ScD	Doctor of Science
SEATO	Southeast Asia Treaty Organization
Sgt	Sergeant
SMP	Statutory Maternity Pay
Sñr	Mr (Spanish)
Sñra	Mrs (Spanish)
Sñrta	Miss (Spanish)
Spett	Messrs (Italian)
Sr	Mr (Italian)
Sra	Mrs (Italian)
Sres	Messrs (Spanish)
Srina	Miss (Italian)
SRL	*société à résponsabilité limitée* (limited liability company)
SRN	State Registered Nurse
SSP	Statutory Sick Pay
tba	to be advised

tbc	to be confirmed
TD	Territorial Decoration
TGWU	Transport and General Workers' Union
TOPS	Training Opportunities
tsvp	*tournez s'il vous plaît* (turn over)
UAE	United Arab Emirates
ult.	ultimo (last)
UNESCO	United National Educational, Scientific and Cultural Organization
UNO	United Nations Organization
VA	Royal Order of Victoria and Albert
VC	Victoria Cross, Vice-Chancellor
VD	Volunteer Officers' Decoration
VDU	visual display unit
Very Revd	Very Reverend
viz.	namely
VP	Vice President
WEDA	Women's Enterprise Development Agency
WHO	World Health Organization
Wing-Cdr	Wing-Commander
WP	word processing
WRAC	Women's Royal Army Corps
WRAF	Women's Royal Air Force
WRNS	Women's Royal Naval Service
WRVS	Women's Royal Voluntary Service
WS	Writer to the Signet
yf	yours faithfully
ys	yours sincerely

WRITING LETTERS ABROAD

As the world shrinks in the face of global electronic and postal communications, so more and more people are travelling abroad, making friends in foreign countries and doing business with other nations. The benefits of this expansion are many: we learn about other cultures and languages; we are able to visit more places; we are able to expand the market for our products and find the best suppliers for our needs.

While children may have pen-friends abroad, their parents may wish to make hotel bookings or travel arrangements. But by far the largest category of people needing to correspond with foreigners is in business. This chapter gives advice on how to deal with foreign languages and cultures when writing letters. Some of the information given is applicable to all forms of letter-writing, but the majority is given with the business correspondent in mind.

Which language should I use?

Many nations of the world use English as the first language, even if their original language is still spoken (India, Sierra Leone, Nigeria, are good examples). However, if this is not the case, you may have to make a decision as to which language to use in correspondence.

This is largely a matter of etiquette and effective communication. For example, if you are sending a mailshot to prospective clients in France, you will probably not get very far if you write in English – very few people will bother to go to the expense of having a mailshot translated. Alternatively, your correspondent may be an old client whom you know to be fluent in English, in which case a communicaion in English is adequate, but not particularly polite.

The general rule, then, is this: write in the language of your correspondent if possible. If not, tailor your English in order to be understood easily.

English as a foreign language

If you opt to carry out your correspondence in English, you will need to simplify your written English so that misunderstandings do not arise. Here are some points to note:

- Avoid idioms that are meaningless if translated literally into the foreign language (going into the red, in the black, raining cats and dogs, etc.).
- Do not use technical jargon.
- Use the correct form of address for the salutation, inside address and envelope address, to ensure that the letter reaches its destination. See p. 149 for some of the forms of address used in foreign languages.
- Write out people's names in full, and use their titles. Correspondents from far afield who are not used to English names may not know whether named people are men or women.
- Do not use abbreviations.
- If you need to mention a body or institution, explain their location and business. Foreigners may not necessarily be familiar with them.
- If you need to mention money, try to give an approximate conversion to the currency of your correspondent as well as a figure in sterling or US dollars. Be careful, however, that you do not commit yourself to a price when you really meant to give merely an idea of costs.
- Write short letters that save your client/supplier money on translation fees.
- A handwritten postscript in the foreign language, perhaps apologising for writing in English, is friendly and may prevent your correspondent thinking you are self-centred.
- Err on the side of formality unless you are well-known to your correspondent.

For information on writing dates in English, see pp. 29-30.

DIVIDED BY A COMMON LANGUAGE

Many countries of the world use English as the language of education, business and law. Some countries use no other language. While these languages are called English, however, they may have important differences that could give rise to costly misunderstandings. The business English of India, for example, is extremely old-fashioned, belonging to a bygone age. The English of the USA, on the other hand, has words that do not appear in British English, or that have a completely different meaning in other English-speaking countries.

The key in all cases is to be aware that any correspondent in a foreign country may use English in a different way, and be prepared to overcome misunderstandings.

Making translations

Unless your own command of the foreign language in question is perfectly fluent, do not attempt to translate your own business letters. (Obviously, if you are writing to a pen-friend, the whole idea may be to improve your knowledge of the language, so mistakes and ambiguities are not important.) If your business is important enough, you will employ a translator to make a translation of your draft.

Most larger towns and cities now have bureaux that can find a translator. Alternatively, you may wish to employ a secretary or personal assistant who is fluent in the language of the country with which you do most business. A third option is to advertise for a translator and employ him or her on a freelance basis. The main advantage with the last two options is that if she works for you over a period of time, your translator will gain an inside knowledge of your business and so understand your correspondence in English, preventing misapprehensions in the translation.

Whoever does your translations, make sure that they are completely fluent, and preferably bi-lingual. A-level standard is not good enough unless there is a wide knowledge of the country's culture, and the etiquette and language of the business world.

When you have found a translator, send her a copy of the completed letter in English, not a first draft or notes. This avoids mistakes in meaning. Going through a first stage in English also means that you will be able to retain an English copy to file next to the foreign version, and you will have a fair copy in English to send to your correspondent along with the translation. Sending both versions is a very good idea, as the English version can act as a failsafe at the other end should there be any misunderstandings.

FOREIGN CHARACTERS

One major advantage of using a professional translator is that he or she will be equipped with a typewriter or word processor that can make the characters specific to the language in question – characters that do not appear in the normal Roman alphabet used in English (e.g. å, ø, ñ). This means that you will not need to invest in this specialized equipment yourself.

Which language?

Some countries use English as the language of business, the law, government, and education, so your correspondence need not be translated. In many other countries, more than one language is spoken.

The following table gives many of the countries of the world, and the language(s) spoken in each.

Country	Official language(s)	Other language(s)
Afghanistan	Pushtu, Dari Persian	
Albania	Albanian	
Algeria	Arabic	French
Andorra	Catalán	French, Spanish
Antigua & Barbuda	English	
Argentina	Spanish	
Australia	English	
Barbados	English	
Belgium	Dutch, French, German	
Belize	English	Spanish
Benin	French	Indigenous languages
Bhutan	Dzonghka	
Bolivia	Spanish, Quechua, Aymara	
Botswana	English, Setswana	
Brazil	Portuguese	
Brunei	Malay, English	Chinese
Bulgaria	Bulgarian	
Burkina Faso	French	Indigenous languages
Myanmar	Burmese	
Burundi	Kirundi	French
Cambodia	Khmer	French, Chinese, Vietnamese
Cameroon	French, English	Indigenous languages
Canada	English, French	
Cape Verde	Portuguese	

Country	Official language(s)	Other language(s)
Central African Republic	French	Sango
Chile	Spanish	
China	Mandarin, Cantonese	Local dialects
Taiwan	Mandarin	Local dialects
Colombia	Spanish	
Comoros	French, Arabic	
Costa Rica	Spanish	
Cuba	Spanish	
Cyprus	Greek, Turkish, English	
Denmark	Danish	
Djibouti	Arabic, French, Afar, Somali, Issa	
Dominica	English	French patois
Dominican Republic	Spanish	
Ecuador	Spanish, Quechua, Jibaro	
Egypt	Arabic	
El Salvador	Spanish	
Ethiopia	Amharic	Galligna, Tigrigna
Fiji	Fijian, Hindustani, English	
Finland	Finnish, Swedish	
France	French	
French Guiana	Creole	
Guadeloupe	French	Creole patois
Martinique	French	Creole patois
Réunion	French	Creole
Gabon	French	Bantu dialects
Gambia	English	Indigenous languages

Country	Official language(s)	Other language(s)
Germany	German	
Ghana	Indigenous languages	English
Greece	Greek	
Grenada	English	
Guatemala	Spanish	Indigenous languages
Guinea	French	Indigenous languages
Guinea-Bissau	Portuguese	
Guyana	English	Hindi, Urdu, Creole
Haiti	French, Creole	
Honduras	Spanish, English in places	Indigenous languages
Hungary	Magyar	
Iceland	Icelandic	
India	Hindi, English	Regional languages
Indonesia	Bahasa Indonesian	Dutch, English, regional languages
Iran	Farsi, Kurdish, Arabic	
Iraq	Arabic, Kurdish	
Ireland, Republic of	English, Irish	
Israel	Hebrew, Arabic, English	
Italy	Italian	
Ivory Coast	French, Indigenous languages	
Jamaica	English	
Japan	Japanese	
Jordan	Arabic, English	
Kenya	Swahili	Bantu, Kikuyu, English

Country	Official language(s)	Other language(s)
Kiribati	English	
Kuwait	Arabic, English	
Laos	Lao	French, English
Lebanon	Arabic	French, English
Lesotho	Sesotho	English
Liberia	English	Indigenous languages
Libya	Arabic	
Liechtenstein	German (dialect)	
Luxembourg	Letzeburgesch, French, German	
Madagascar	Malagasy, French	
Malawi	English	Chichewa
Malaysia	Malay	Chinese, Tamil, English
Maldives	Divehi	
Mali	French	Indigenous languages
Malta	Maltese, English	
Mauritania	Arabic, French	
Mauritius	English	French, Creole, Hindi, Urdu, Chinese
Mexico	Spanish	Indigenous languages
Monaco	French, Monégasque, Italian	
Mongolia	Mongolian	
Morocco	Arabic, French, Spanish	
New Zealand	English, Maori	
Nicaragua	Spanish	
Niger	French	Hausa, Songhai, Arabic

Country	Official language(s)	Other language(s)
Nigeria	English	Regional languages
Norway	Norwegian	
Oman	Arabic	
Pakistan	Urdu, English	Regional languages
Panama	Spanish	
Papua New Guinea	English, Melanesian pidgin	Indigenous dialects
Paraguay	Spanish	Guarani
Peru	Spanish, Quechua	
Philippines	Filipino, English, Spanish	Local languages
Poland	Polish	
Portugal	Portuguese	
Qatar	Arabic	
Romania	Romanian, Hungarian, Serbian, German, Turkish	
Rwanda	Kinyarwanda, French	
St Lucia	English	Patois
San Marino	Italian	
Saudi Arabia	Arabic	
Senegal	French	Indigenous languages
Seychelles	Creole	English, French
Sierra Leone	English	Mende, Temne, Creole
Singapore	Malay, Mandarin, Tamil, English	
Solomon Islands	English	Indigenous languages
Somalia	Somali, Arabic	English, Italian
South Africa	English, Afrikaans	Bantu languages

Country	Official language(s)	Other language(s)
Spain	Castilian	Basque, Catalán, Galician
Sri Lanka	Sinhala, Tamil, English	
Sudan	Arabic, English	Indigenous dialects
Surinam	Dutch	Surinamese
Swaziland	Swazi	English
Sweden	Swedish	
Switzerland	German, French, Italian, Romansch	
Syria	Arabic	
Tanzania	Swahili, Arabic, English	
Thailand	Thai, Chinese, English	
Tonga	English, Tongan	
Trinidad & Tobago	English	Hindi
Tunisia	Arabic, French	
Turkey	Turkish	
Tuvalu	Tuvaluan, English	
Uganda	English	Swahili, other indigenous languages
United Arab Emirates	Arabic	
Uruguay	Spanish	
Venezuela	Spanish	
Vietnam	Vietnamese	
Yemen	Arabic	
Zaire	French	Bantu dialects
Zambia	English	Indigenous dialects
Zimbabwe	English	Ndebele, Shona

Taking account of customs and culture

Successful interaction with people of foreign countries depends on your ability to take into account their ways of thinking and doing things. Some nationalities are extremely formal in their business dealings, whereas others (notably the Americans) like to be on first-name terms right from the start.

If you are considering entering a foreign market for the first time, it is wise to read up on the society you are hoping to be dealing with. For example, some of the Oriental cultures lay a great deal of stress on the concept of 'face' – being made to back down, or lose face, is degrading, and if you put a client or supplier in this situation, your business dealings are likely to flounder. Equally, in many Middle Eastern cultures, business can be carried out very slowly (sometimes agonizingly so), and an impatient business partner will simply alienate his or her Middle Eastern correspondents.

A short spell of homework will mean you are aware of these cultural differences, and enable you to avoid making socially unacceptable blunders, especially when dealing at arm's length through written correspondence.

Forms of address for foreign countries

Whether you are writing in English or a foreign language, it is desirable that you get the address and salutation correct, so that the letter reaches the correct destination and you strike the right level of formality at the outset.

If writing in English, take advice on a foreign-language salutation, to make a good impression at the start. You may also find the information you need in letters you have received from overseas.

When addressing the envelope, be sure to follow the layout given on your correspondent's letterhead or envelope. When writing from the UK, always write the name of the country in English. When writing from abroad, always write the name of the country in the language of the country you are in.

Here are foreign-language titles for some of our European neighbours:

English	Mr	Mrs	Miss	Messrs	c/o
Italian	Sr	Sra	Srina	Spett.	presso Ditta
French	M	Mme	Mlle	MM	chez
German	Herr	Frau	Fraulein	Firma	bei
Spanish	Sñr	Sñra	Sñrta	Sres	supplicada en casa de

See also: pp. 10-11 on paper for airmail; pp. 250-51 for writing letters home from abroad; pp. 291-3 for writing to a pen pal abroad.

THE LAW ON LETTER WRITING

Just as our physical behaviour towards one another is regulated by the legal system, so too are the letters we write. It is very important, therefore that what is contained in a letter does not break the law, either through intention or through carelessness.

Letter writing is governed by a number of laws, either specifically (as in the case of the Malicious Communications Act, which regulates the type of mail permitted), or generally (e.g. the Copyright Act can cover letters). This chapter looks at the kind of trouble likely to arise from what is contained in a letter, and how to avoid it.

Making your mark

A signature on any document is considered in law to mean that you understand what is contained in it and that you are in agreement with it. Most people realize that once a letter is signed, they may be held responsible for its contents, even if the contents have not been read.

Employer's responsibility

In the business context, the law goes a little further than this. In some cases it also assigns responsibility to the employer for letters signed in the employer's absence, or written and signed by an employee in the course of his or her work. The law considers the employee to be acting with the employer's permission when letters are sent out, even if such permission were not expressly given, but the employee had good reason to believe that the letter was called for as part of the job.

No employer can read and approve every letter that leaves the office, but he or she can make employees aware of the legalities concerning letter-writing.

Defamation

Defamation is any communication to a third party that is to the detriment of a person's reputation, his goods or work, or his ownership of something. Slander is defamation by word of mouth. Libel is defamation by a more permanent method of communication, such as radio and television broadcasts, newspaper articles or letters. For a letter to be libellous it must:

- Be 'published' to a third party.
- Be malicious in intent.
- Appear to be factual in content.
- Tend to slur the reputation of the subject in the minds of 'right-thinking people'.

There are some cases when it is in the interests of your correspondent to pass on information that may be to the subject's detriment: perhaps you have been asked to write a reference, for example, and would like to warn the correspondent not to employ the subject. There are some instances when it is permissible to write ill of a person without being in breach of the libel laws. However, always consider very carefully before starting on a letter of this kind. Try to satisfy the following criteria:

- Are your facts true and provable?
- Can the passing of this information be justified as being in the public interest?
- Is the substance of your letter really only your opinion?
- Can the substance of your letter be called 'fair comment'?

It is not enough that your facts are true and provable. You must be able to show that you revealed them to the third party because it was in the public interest. For example, you may feel compelled to write a reference that calls a former employee a thief and a liar. These are very serious allegations. Make sure that you can argue that you intended to do some good by relaying this information to the third party, and search your heart for any sign of malicious intent. If you intend to do the subject harm, you will almost certainly be sued.

Your letter may give opinions rather than facts, and if this is the case, you should make this clear, and ensure that you can justify 'publishing' these opinions as a fair comment upon the facts.

Publication

You may at some stage feel compelled to use harsh words in a letter to the subject himself. Be careful: while a letter containing accusations or libellous words addressed for the subject's eyes only may not have been intended for publication to a third party, you may find that the company mail clerk or the recipient's secretary has opened and perused the letter. This constitutes publication, even though the letter read in this way was not intended for anyone but the subject.

If you wish to send a letter of this nature, make doubly sure that it is marked 'Strictly private and personal'. Mark the envelope and the top of the letter. Take a photocopy of both to prove that you did everything you could to ensure that the letter was not published.

Negligence

It may be that you are asked to give a correspondent information. Always be careful to check the facts thoroughly, or you could be liable for negligence.

Under the law, each person owes a 'duty of care' to every other person. If you give a person information, and he or she acts on it believing it to be true, and then suffers losses because the information turns out to be incorrect, you may very well be sued. The court will consider you to have been negligent, even if you or your company have not been paid for the information or advice.

Malicious communications

The law expressly forbids certain types of letter or communication. Therefore, never send out communications or materials that could be considered:

- Threatening.
- Grossly indecent.
- Deliberately false.
- Or grossly offensive.

Letters in disputes

When entering a dispute, always consider that your letters, actions and words may eventually land up in court. Ensure that your words are ones of reason, that they are not libellous, and, most of all, that your facts are correct.

If a dispute escalates and eventually you resort to the law (or your correspondent does), you will be ordered to make your correspondence available to both the prosecution and the defence, even that which may be detrimental to your own case. Therefore:

- Keep copies of all letters you send.
- Keep the letters you receive.
- Make a diary of the events in the dispute, especially of telephone calls, meetings or actions.
- Never write in the heat of your fury, but temper your message with reason.
- Send letters by recorded delivery.

See also pp. 201-2 for examples of letters written during disputes.

Proof of posting/proof of delivery

There may be a number of occasions on which you would like to be able to prove that an important letter reached its destination. A document showing that the letter was posted does not automatically prove that the letter was delivered. You will need to use a service such as the Royal Mail's recorded delivery, or a reputable courier firm that collects signatures on delivery.

However, it is still good practice to keep a detailed list of the mail that leaves your premises. In the absence of a signature of delivery, a mail book that is kept systematically will go a long way towards proving in court that a letter was sent.

At the other end, a postmark will prove beyond doubt the date of posting, and, if you can show you are consistent in your use of date-stamps for incoming mail (see pp. 115-16), this will be enough to prove the date of receipt.

Contracts

The question of dates of posting and receipt is most relevant when your correspondence involves the negotiation of a contract. A contract can be made orally or on paper, but it must have the following characteristics:

- There must be an unconditional offer.
- There must be unconditional acceptance.
- There must be some kind of exchange or 'consideration'.
- The contract's terms must be enforceable in law.

Unconditional offer

A catering firm offers to cater a wedding reception at a certain price per head, depending on the type of food and amount of drink required. This offer is conditional. To make it unconditional, the caterer would need to describe the exact catering requirements, and give a price.

Unconditional acceptance

The mother of the bride accepts the unconditional offer made by the caterers to supply food and drink of a certain type, but makes it clear that she will need to discuss this with her husband, who is footing the bill. This acceptance is conditional upon the husband agreeing. Once he has agreed, and that fact has been conveyed to the caterer, the acceptance becomes unconditional and a contract can be said to have been entered into.

Consideration

However, if friends have been asked to take care of the catering, out of the goodness of their hearts, and no exchange of money or goods is mentioned, there is no contract.

Enforceable in law

If the contract is agreed but can later be shown to be missing some vital element, it can also be said to be void. For example, you may have ordered some goods, but failed to state how many, or how much. In this case the contract cannot work, because it is missing a term, and is so 'untenable in law'.

Equally, if a contract contains terms that are illegal or excluded by the law, the contract can be said to be void.

Negotiating contracts

When writing letters negotiating a contract (and you should always set out the terms in a letter or legal document, rather than leaving them in an oral agreement), be careful not to make unconditional acceptance before you are ready. Always make it perfectly clear whether you are ready to enter into a contract.

Always read the small print. If you accept an offer that includes small print, you may find that the terms contained in it are not to your liking. Too late – the contract has already been made, and you will not be released from it, especially if you have already taken delivery of the goods in question.

The stages of the negotiating of a contract are important. If the offeror makes an unconditional offer and then needs to amend the terms, he cannot do so after the offer has been accepted. For these purposes, the date and time of the acceptance are important.

It is permissible to accept an offer by telex, because the telex process enables the correspondent to prove that the message was received. It is also permissible to accept an offer by mail (but get a signature as proof of delivery). Facsimile is a less tried method, and is still a grey area in the law because there is no proof that the message sent was received complete and in a legible form. However, as the technology improves further, and more cases pass through the courts, the situation will no doubt become more clear.

Copyright

Copyright law ensures that the person who creates a work is entitled to be its owner. A letter received by you automatically becomes yours, but its content remains the property of the author. This type of property is known as 'intellectual property' and includes ideas, writing, images, designs, etc. So if you wish to publish the contents of someone's letter to you, you will need to get permission to do so. Copyright exists in the contents of the letter until fifty years after the author's death.

There is one major exception to this rule. Employees who produce intellectual property in the course of their paid work have no title to the ownership of that property unless their contract of employment expressly says so. The ownership of this work lies with the employer.

Without prejudice

These enigmatic words appear on many letters in negotiations. Essentially they mean that what appears in the letter does not form any part of the negotiation unless it is completed successfully. A businesswoman negotiates a deal, and in the process of doing so, makes a number of concessions. Eventually the deal breaks down, and so none of the concessions made can be held to be binding. However, if the deal succeeds, the concessions cease to be protected, and become part of the contract unless superseded in the correspondence.

The Data Protection Act

With advances in technology, it is now possible for companies to store the personal information of large numbers of people on computer disk for use in mailing lists or for other reasons. Information given when filling in forms may be used in this way. Under the Data Protection Act, every individual has a right of access to information stored in this way. Those holding the information must register with a central body, and have a duty to keep the information confidential (apart from authorized use) and correct.

So there are many legal elements to writing letters, but if you are honest and fair you will not fall foul of the law, especially if you follow these guidelines:

- Always check that your facts are correct to the best of your knowledge.
- Ensure that nothing you have said will harm another person's reputation.
- Send important letters by recorded delivery.
- Never sign a letter or other document without first reading it carefully.
- Make sure that your words are unambiguous.
- Make sure that those writing letters on your behalf understand that what they write must follow the same guidelines.

LETTERS
FOR ALL
OCCASIONS

ACCEPTING A POSITION

When you have been offered a job, it is usual to write to the new employer, formally accepting the position. Thanks are obviously in order, but avoid appearing too grovellingly grateful. Include the details of the job as you understand them. This is not useless repetition, but gives your prospective employer an opportunity to ensure that there is no confusion.

If the vacancy was handled by the company's personnel office, it is appropriate to write to the Personnel Officer rather than the person for whom you will be working. You should of course respond to a job offer as soon as possible, if not by return.

This letter is best typed, and should be set out as a formal business letter. See the sample letter on p. 39 showing fully-blocked style with corresponding open punctuation.

Dear Mrs Warren

Your Offer of Position as Quality Control Officer
Thank you for your letter of 20th January. I am pleased to accept your offer of the post of Quality Control Officer.

I understand that working hours are 8.30 a.m.–4.30 p.m., with one hour for lunch. The starting salary of £12,500 p.a. will be reviewed after a three-month probationary period.

I confirm that I will be free to start work at 8.30 a.m. on 1st February, and will contact you on arrival. I look forward to becoming a member of the team.

Yours sincerely

ACKNOWLEDGMENTS

There is no better way to lose business than to allow a letter to remain unanswered. Even if you are trying to keep your head above the flood waters of the busy season, acknowledging the receipt of a letter is polite and looks efficient. Acknowledgments can also be used to obtain further information to speed the relationship along.

Simple acknowledgments of the receipt of a letter (an enquiry, perhaps, or an order or application) can be printed on postcards and addressed using sticky labels, or on A5 headed paper (a short message such as these would look terse on A4). If using postcards, remember to have them printed with your company's name and address. Here are some possible wordings:

'Thank you for your order of ... (date). Your goods will be despatched within 28 days.'

'Thank you for your application for the position of ... This has been passed to Personnel for consideration. We hope to respond to all applications for this post within a fortnight.'

'Thank you for your enquiry of ... (date). This has been passed to ... (department/executive name), and you should receive a response within a week.'

'We are pleased to say that the items that you ordered are now in stock. We will hold them for collection for two weeks, and look forward to seeing you.'

As these examples show, it is extremely helpful to give the timescale for receipt of a response.

Acknowledgments that also include requests for further information could make use of standard sentences and space for further comments:

Dear Sir/Madam

Thank you for your order of ... (date). We are, however, unable to despatch your goods at once for the following reasons:

[ ] You have omitted to state the quantity required.
[ ] You have omitted to state the model numbers.
[ ] Please send remittance of £...
[ ] Your cheque has not been signed.
[ ] See notes below.

Yours faithfully

Dear Sir/Madam

We are processing your request for ... In order to make it possible for us to do this quickly, please send further documentation as follows:

[ ] Completed form A103 (enclosed).
[ ] Completed form A104 (enclosed).
[ ] Two passport-sized photographs, each signed on the back.
[ ] See notes below:

Yours faithfully

The sentences that do not apply can be crossed out as necessary, or the relevant sentences can be ticked using the boxes given. Relevant documentation can be enclosed. A space at the end of the form could be used for handwritten notes to convey a message not covered in the standard responses.

See **Notes for Office Workers** pp. 111-12, for further information on saving time by using standard letters.

APOLOGIES

There are some occasions when there is no getting round it – you are in the wrong. You may have made a complaint that turns out to be unfounded, or you may have failed to do something you promised to do, or done something you promised not to do. Whatever the situation, it is wise to make the apology immediately, or as soon as possible after you find out that apologies are in order. Probably the best way to do this is by letter – it is so much easier to apologize on paper than in person.

The way to word an apology depends on the exact situation, but try to avoid abject grovelling, and flimsy excuses. Try to sound sincere, and, where necessary, be prepared to take full responsibility.

Letters of apology are best written in the formal style, using the title and surname, and signing with 'Yours sincerely'.

Perhaps you have requested a customer to pay a debt that is not due:

> Dear Mr Wright
>
> Thank you for your letter of 15th January. I have looked back in our records, and find that it was we who were in error, and not you. I see that your account is paid up to date, for which many thanks.
>
> The error may have arisen when our book-keeper was on holiday, and a temporary was providing cover. Please accept my apologies for having troubled you.
>
> Yours sincerely

This letter is courteous and brief. It offers a plausible explanation and offers apologies. It may not be ideal, however, because the writer is blaming a temporary book-keeper for the error.

Perhaps you have failed to send some information that you agreed to supply:

> Dear Mr Wright
>
> You may remember that when we last met I offered to send you details of our D2 model computer. I have been looking back at our records and see that I failed to make a note, and so have not yet sent you the information.
>
> I am enclosing the brochure, which should give you the details you require to make a decision. Please accept my apologies for this oversight. I hope the delay has not inconvenienced you.
>
> Yours sincerely

In this letter, the writer admits that he failed to do something he said he would, even though there are no extraordinary circumstances. He takes full responsibility, he is quick to put the problem right and show that he is thinking of how his oversight has inconvenienced his customer.

In personal life, you may have received a complaint from a neighbour:

> *Dear Mrs Wright,*
>
> *Thank you for your letter. I am sorry that you have been disturbed by my radio. I am hard of hearing and so need to have it turned up fairly loud. I did not realize it could be heard outside the house.*
>
> *I will, of course, be sure to turn the radio down or off late in the evenings as you suggest, but if I am still disturbing you, please let me know and I will consider some other action.*
>
> *My apologies once again for disturbing you.*
>
> *Yours sincerely,*

This letter is ideal for an action that was unwittingly causing offence. The writer has a good reason for turning the radio up, but is prepared to compromise. Her apologies are courteous.

More serious apologies are in order when something has happened, even by accident, that has caused harm rather than inconvenience or annoyance. In the following letter, a neighbour's tree-pruning activities have led to destruction of property:

Dear Mrs Jones

I must immediately apologize for the state of your garden fence, which I am afraid, was my fault.

While you were away I decided that the oak tree needed to be pruned to stop it causing any harm this winter. While I was up in the branches, one very large branch, which appeared to have been dead, fell and crushed your fence.

I have cleared the debris, and will, of course, pay to have the fence rebuilt as soon as possible. Please let me know when it would be convenient for me to discuss this with you.

Please accept my apologies. This must be very inconvenient for you.

Yours sincerely

The writer has made an immediate apology, and has accepted full responsibility. He has explained the circumstances of the accident, and, while it was not strictly his fault, he has offered to make amends.

It is important in these cases to show that you understand the gravity of the situation. You must also show that you are willing to do everything you can to put the matter right.

APPEALS AND FUNDRAISING

At some time, you may be called upon to raise money for a charity or for a club or society, and persuading people to part with their cash is not an easy business, however worthy the cause. If your request is made by post, it may be even more difficult to influence people to give generously – we are all much more likely to consign a begging letter to the waste-paper basket without a second thought, than say 'no' to a personal caller with a collecting tin.

Your fundraising letter will need to overcome a number of pitfalls and obstacles before it can be successful in its aims. The first obstacle is the addressee's interest. The letter must invite attention and make the reader continue reading far enough for you to get your point across. The overall presentation and the first paragraph of the letter are therefore very important. Second, you must avoid the pitfalls of unnecessary information when describing your 'project'. Third, you must tell the addressee how he or she will benefit from the 'project' – why anyone should bother sending a donation. Fourth, and perhaps most importantly, you must spur the reader to action.

Opening

The first few words of the letter serve to grab the reader's attention. This is vital if the letter is to be a success. Use a headline, similar to a subject heading (see **Layout and Component Parts** p. 33). If you have a word processor, enhance the words or use a larger typesize to make them stand out. You may choose to use just the name of the fund, or you may go for something more like a newspaper headline:

Paddox CAT-scan Appeal
Save St Margaret's Fighting Fund
Smith Family Fund

or:
Hopewell Bridge is Falling Down!

Getting the information across

Remember the advice given in the earlier part of this book, and you won't go far wrong in choosing the most important facts and arranging them so that the message is clear. Where a fundraising letter may differ from other letters is in the use of sentences to punctuate the information, to startle the reader into attentiveness or make the letter more dynamic. In this way you can also highlight the most important words. (Using enhancements such as italic, bold and underline will do the same job.)

Don't try to put too much in. If you have information that is interesting but not vital to the message, put it in a separate leaflet or information sheet, but don't forget to mention it in the letter.

Mention the benefit to the donor

We are all human, and most of us are a little selfish. If we are told there is to be some benefit to us we are more likely to give money. The benefits could be seen in many different ways: a better environment; a quieter life; the pleasure of knowing we have helped the less fortunate; our names inscribed on a public roll to show others how generous we are; a better education for our children. Whatever the benefit (and you should be able to show at least one), mention it, and if you can, repeat it, so that it becomes lodged in the reader's mind.

Action line

Finally, all there is left is to tell the recipient how to become a donor, what to do to pass over the money or make the promise of sponsorship. Keep it simple – a short form typed at the foot of the letter for the name, address and amount is all that is required. Don't forget to add the address for donations to the form (letters often become detached from forms and vital information such as this is lost).

Urge the reader to do it immediately before your letter is placed on a dusty pile and forgotten. Immediately means today, now, this minute, right away. Use word like these to goad your reader to action.

Dear Member

Cycling the Sahara
We all know Chris and Susie Smith, active members of our society for many years, and big-time cycling enthusiasts. It seems that Chris and Susie are planning a trip – a long trip cycling across the Sahara in aid of the society's Kurdish Children Appeal.

They will not be cycling for fun.

They will be doing it for money – your money.
Chris and Susie need you to sponsor them to cycle the breadth of the Sahara. Why? So that we can help keep Kurdish children alive and well.

Sponsor the Smiths today to complete this gruelling trip (details of the journey are enclosed).

Susie will document the journey photographically, and a bound album will be presented to the society. Anyone who promises more than £100 will have their name inscribed in the album for posterity. And everyone who makes a donation will receive the silent thanks of all the Kurdish children we are able to help.

Make your vows now! Fill in the form and return it to me today.

Yours sincerely

ASSOCIATIONS AND SOCIETIES

The secretary of an association or society is burdened with a number of letter-writing duties: writing to the press with details of activities (see pp. 261-6); circulating details of activities or requests for volunteer help or new members; or even booking venues, speakers and caterers.

Any letters written on behalf of the society should always bear the letterhead of the society. Alternatively use your private address with the name of the society above and using the letters c/o:

Singertown Operatic Society
c/o 24 Frederick Mews
Singertown
(0076) 098765

You should sign yourself in your capacity as secretary to make it clear that you are not acting as a private person:

Yours sincerely

Belinda Singer (Mrs)
Secretary

Lay the letter out as you would a business letter, rather than as a personal letter (see p. 39).

Notices of activities and meetings

Routine notices of meetings and activities can be typed out once and then photocopied, or word processed as a standard letter. If you begin 'Dear Member', you will not need to add the member's name, but if you do have time to write in members' names, leave out the salutation from the typed version of the letter and write it in yourself. This gives the letter a more friendly tone.

You might also like to have the mailing list photocopied onto sticky labels to reduce the time spent writing out addresses. (See pp. 48-9 on standard letters.)

Notices of this type are usually sent out once in a while, and include details of all activities for that period. In this case, a friendly covering letter with a detailed list enclosed should do the trick.

Singertown Operatic Society
c/o 24 Frederick Mews
Singertown
(0076) 098765
10th September 1995

Dear Member

Welcome back. I hope everyone had a good summer break.

This year, we have a large number of activities lined up, as well as our annual major production, which is *The Mikado*. The highlight of the year will be our 25th anniversary celebrations in June, which will include concerts, a weekend workshop, an exhibition and a gala performance of *The Mikado*.

We have also organized a good number of social events and visits to the opera, which I hope you will support and enjoy. Details of all the activities arranged so far are given on the enclosed schedule.

We could not undertake any of these activities without your continued enthusiastic support, and a great deal of hard work. I hope you will continue to support us as in the past. We hope to see you and any new members at 7.30 p.m. on Thursday 25th September at the Parish Church Hall, for a welcome back drink, followed by some first thoughts on the main production.

We look forward to seeing you there.

Yours sincerely

Belinda Singer (Mrs)
Secretary
Enc.

This letter is friendly and welcoming. It gives a sense of continuity and community, and takes time to highlight the interesting activities in store. It reminds existing members that they are welcome to bring prospective new members along, but a full membership drive should ideally be kept for a separate letter.

Call for members

New members are the lifeblood of any society. Their subscriptions increase the number of activities a society can undertake, and the presence of new people prevents the social aspect of the society becoming stale. After all, one of the reasons many people join a society is to meet new people.

Membership drives require what are essentially selling letters. You will need to make your society's activities sound appealing and worthwhile in order to grab a potential member's interest. Consider the following points:

- Is the society small or large?
- Is membership restricted?

- Are you looking for people with certain skills?
- Are you looking for people in certain age-groups?
- Are your activities expensive or cheap?
- Is the social aspect of your society uppermost, or do you put more emphasis on activities?
- Does the society have any successes that have been publicized recently?
- Does membership require absolute commitment, or is it possible to be a member without devoting all one's free time to activities?

When you have a good idea of the type of people you would like to apply for membership, you will need to work out how your message is to reach them. Consider what interests they share with your members, and where they might go in pursuit of these. In the case of the Singertown Operatic Society, a poster in the music section at the local library might bring results, or if you are looking for younger members, you might circulate the head teachers at local schools and colleges. You might alert the press (see pp. 264-6), or you might ask existing members to find potential members among friends, relatives or workmates.

The following letter is for circulation at local schools and colleges, seeking young new members for the conservation society.

Dear Mr Hardcastle

Fieldview Conservation Society Membership Drive
Last summer a number of members from Fieldview Conservation Society took part in the revitalization of Fieldview Ponds. The project was supervised by John Beale, the television conservation expert, and the work of our members was featured on local television and radio.

Fieldview Conservation Society is seeking new members to help us build on the success of the Ponds project.
Our activities are many and diverse. They include:

- Nature walks
- Talks/slide-shows by well-known conservationists
- Conservation projects
- Visits to exhibitions and conservation events

We are seeking new members who are interested in any area of conservation, from natural history to practical projects to clean, enhance and protect the natural environment.

Prospective members are invited to an introductory evening, to meet existing members and hear about our plans for the coming year. This will take place on 15th September 1994 at Fieldview School, starting at 7.30 p.m.

I do hope to see some of your students there.

Yours sincerely

This letter begins by describing a success story, implying that new members can expect to be involved in similarly successful projects should they choose to join. It goes on to list the wide range of activities on offer and gives the time and place for the meeting. By sending it to the headmaster of a local school, the writer hopes to reach young people who are interested in natural history and conservation.

Request for a speaker

Some societies invite speakers to visit the society and give a talk to members. The secretary may be asked to find suitable speakers and arrange a visit.

Finding a speaker

Some societies frequently find speakers from among their own ranks. The advantage is that you rarely have to pay a speaker who is also a member. However, the disadvantage is that you may find your speaker is not up to the job. Public speaking can be nerve-wracking for many people, and unless trained to do this kind of thing (for example, teachers), or well-practised, you may end up with a very embarrassing evening.

On the other hand it is relatively easy to find professionals in your society's field who would be more than willing to give a slide show, lecture or informal talk. One of the society's members may have heard a speaker at a function, and recommend him or her, or a journalist or writer in your field may also have a sideline in public speaking. If your field is covered by a national association, they may have a list of experts who are willing to speak. (A list of national societies and associations can be found in Whitacker's *Almanack*).

When you have settled upon a particular speaker, try to arrange to hear him or her speak at another function, so that you are sure you have chosen the right person. Some people are admirably qualified in their field, but, through no fault of their own, are not very good speakers. Alternatively, get a personal recommendation.

Invitation to speak

The first approach should be by letter. As with other society correspondence, write in your official capacity, using the society's letterhead if you can.

Give the following information:

- How you found the speaker.
- The kind of 'talk' you are expecting (with slide show/ lecture/demonstration).
- A few details about the society, including membership to assure the speaker that he/she would be well-received by an audience of more than ten.

- Roughly the time you were thinking of scheduling the meeting.
- Mention a fee. Some speakers charge fees, others do not. Always be prepared to pay travel expenses in any case. You might also find yourself booking overnight accommodation if the speaker has to travel a long distance.

Dear Mr Foulkes

One of our members heard you speak last week on traditional textile production in India, and enjoyed the evening very much. I was wondering whether you would be able to find time to visit us to give a talk with a slide show if possible.

Highdale Craft Society has nearly 70 members, all of whom practise a handicraft. Many of us have read of your work, and we would be delighted if you were to pay us a visit.

We meet on Tuesday evenings at the Town Hall, but would arrange a special meeting if this day does not suit you. Please let me know what kind of fee you charge.

Yours sincerely

You may need to enter into other correspondence to book and confirm speaking arrangements. *Collins Pocket Reference Speaking in Public* gives further information.

(See also pp. 289-90 for a letter of thanks to a visiting speaker, and pp. 261-6 for how to publicize your society's activities.

BON VOYAGE

In these days of global mobility, many people have friends who are planning a lengthy trip abroad, either for business or pleasure.

It is not necessary to send a bon voyage message to people who are taking their two-week annual vacation, unless you have a particular reason to make contact. However, cards and letters to those who are embarking on more lengthy trips are much appreciated in those apprehensive days before departure.

The best way to send this message is with a decorated greetings card. To make your communication truly personal, chose a card that is blank inside.

Start your message as you would a personal letter (Dear Nicky), or write it as you would a postcard, without a salutation.

What to say? Here are some ideas:

- How exciting embarking on the trip must be.
- How much the person will be missed.
- Remind the person about the lot of those left behind.
- A quip about the pain of vaccinations.
- A comment on the size of the business traveller's expense account.
- Exhort the person to keep well/keep out of trouble.
- Wish their business success.
- Exhort the person to write (add your full address).
- Finish with the words Bon Voyage.

Dear Nicky & Godfrey,
   Two years in Japan is a very long time. I will, of course miss you both very much.
   I know you will be busy when you get there, but as soon as

you are settled in, write and let me know what life is like over there. I may even have to find an excuse to come and visit.

Remember the good times in this gloomy city, and come back to us in two whole pieces.

Bon Voyage, and every success,

Love,

It is appropriate to write some time in the ten days before the planned departure. Replies are not normally required.

See also **Letters Home**.

BOOKINGS

There are several occasions on which you may be called upon to make a booking: a hotel for a holiday or short break; a venue for a function such as a wedding reception or Christmas party. You will normally need to go through two stages. First is the enquiry stage, and second is the booking stage. At the second stage you will be making a contract based on the information you have received. So read the section on pp. 154-6 about the legalities of making a contract.

Finding out

It is rarely wise to book accommodation or a venue without having enough information to make the booking. The following letter, laid out as a business letter, is an enquiry about booking a restaurant for a Christmas party:

Dear Sir

Christmas Catering
Our company is looking for a restaurant to cater for our staff Christmas party on an evening in the week of Christmas Eve.

Please let me know whether you would be prepared to cater for a party of about 25. I would be grateful if you would also send details of any special set menu you are planning for Christmas, price per head and your deposit requirements.

Yours faithfully

The next letter is a preliminary enquiry to a hotel:

Dear Sir

A friend stayed with you last year and has recommended the hotel to me.

Please let me know how much two nights' weekend bed and

breakfast accommodation would be for two adults and one child (aged two). Also, the price for full board. We would like to come one weekend in June.

Do you permit pets? We would like to bring our Labrador with us.

I hope to hear from you shortly,

Yours faithfully

Making the booking

It is important when you make a booking to repeat the terms of the booking as you understand them. Include the date(s), the price, the number of people, and all other relevant details. This acts as a double check for the establishment involved and sets out the terms of your contract with it.

Dear Mr Rice

Booking
Thank you for responding to my enquiry regarding our staff Christmas party so promptly.

I would like to reserve tables for 24 people for the evening of Thursday, 22nd December. We will choose from the set menu you describe in your letter of 10th December, at a price of £12.50 per head (inclusive of VAT and service).

I am enclosing a deposit of £50 as requested. I understand that this sum is non-returnable unless the cancellation is made more than 10 days in advance. The balance of the bill will be paid by company cheque at the end of the evening.

We expect to arrive at 7.30 p.m. I look forward to seeing you then.

Yours sincerely

The reservation should be confirmed in writing by the restaurant, and checked by telephone on the day of the function or the day before.

> Dear Mrs Smith
>
> Reservation
> Thank you for your letter of 24th February 1994.
>
> Please would you reserve a double room for myself, my husband and 2-year-old child (who will require an extra cot), for Friday 22nd June 1994 to Sunday 24th June inclusive (2 nights bed and breakfast). Please also reserve kennel space for our Labrador.
> I understand that the cost will be £40 per night + VAT, breakfast included, for the room, and an extra £7 per night + VAT for the kennel and dog food.
>
> I am enclosing a cheque for £20 as a non-returnable deposit against cancellation.
>
> We will probably arrive late afternoon on 22nd June, and I look forward to meeting you then.
>
> Yours sincerely

When writing a letter booking a venue or accommodation, remember to include the following details as you understand them:

- Day, date and time of arrival.
- Type of accommodation/catering required.
- Cost details.
- Details of any taxes, services charges or any other extras to the cost.
- Amount and details of deposit enclosed (returnable? non-returnable?).
- Method of payment of the balance if appropriate.

If you are unsure of any of the details of the service offered, do not make the booking until your questions are answered unequivocally.

CHANGE OF ADDRESS

One of the many things to be done when moving house or office, is to inform friends, colleagues, customers and relatives of your new address.

By far the best way to do this is to send out postcards with the information. You may even wish to have a number of postcards printed professionally. For a home address you will need to include the following information:

- The words 'change of address'.
- Your name.
- The new address including the postcode. You will be able to find out the postcode from the Royal Mail's postcode information service.
- The new telephone number/fax number as applicable.
- The date from which the new address takes effect.

Change of Address
Andrews & Co
is moving to new premises at
26 Corporation Street
London EC9 8AD
Telephone and fax numbers remain the same
With effect from 1st November 1994

Change of Address
On 20th June Charlotte and Drew Phillips
are moving to a new address:

156 Anglesey Road
Newtown NT5 6TF
Tel: 0987–04532

Even if you are very organized, and have managed to send your change of address cards out in good time, you might wish to take advantage of the Royal Mail's redirection service, to catch letters that have slipped through the net. This way you can have mail redirected by the Post Office to your new address, and so avoid missing correspondence.

If you are in business, you might wish to save on postage and send out standard letters along with selling material. In this case, make sure any enclosures give the new address, and not the old one, to avoid confusion.

Another chore to be done when moving is to have personalized stationery or company letterheads brought up to date. If you still have a large amount of stationery that carries the old address, you might like to have small stickers printed with the new address, so that you can attach them to the old stationery and avoid wastage.

CLASSIFIED ADVERTISEMENTS

Many newspapers and magazines carry classified advertisements. They can cover classifications as diverse as woodworm
control services and lonely hearts.

Which publication?

If you decide to place an advert in the classifieds, the first
point to consider is the publication you would like to use.
Every publication has a slightly different market. Some (like
local newspapers) are of interest to people living in the locality. Others (such as specialist magazines) are bought by people
with something in common, be it an industry, a hobby or an
interest.

If you have a piece of furniture to sell, you may simply
choose to use the local newspaper. But if that piece is an
antique of some value, you may find a buyer through a specialist antiques magazine. If you are offering a general business service, such as typing, the local newspaper will bring
local clients. However, if you are marketing a computer training service, you may again wish to look for an industry or
other specialist magazine.

Bear in mind the cost of the advert. In general, newspapers
are cheaper than magazines. The advert may even be free if
your goods for sale are under a certain price.

Choosing a classification

Most publications that have large classified advert sections
will give a list of classifications, making it a simple matter of
choosing the title that suits your needs.

Classifications normally fall into the following general
categories:

- Recruitment (people advertising for staff and those looking for jobs).
- Education (training courses, private tutors, etc.).
- Property (houses and flats to let or for sale, garages, land, etc.).
- Leisure (holidays, party equipment and venues, sports, etc.).
- Articles for sale and articles wanted.
- Personal (lonely hearts, marriage and dating agencies, personal services).
- Domestic services (builders, domestic appliances, garden supplies, DIY supplies, etc.).

When considering the classification, try to place the advert in the classification most likely to be read by a person you hope would reply. For example, if you have a sunbed for sale, you may chose to place it in the section headed electrical appliances, and not in the section devoted to suntanning services.

Type of ad

Advertisements are categorized according to the form in which they appear in print: lineage (usually the cheapest), semi-display and display (the most expensive).

Lineage

This is the basic style of advert. The line is a column wide, and the print is quite small. The first couple of words of your text are given in bold.

ARMCHAIR brown leather,
good condition, must be seen
£45. Tel: 654326.

Semi-display

A semi-display advert is usually the same width as a lineage advert, but has a box placed round it (with text centred inside) to mark it out from lineage adverts.

```
+-----------------------------------+
|            ARMCHAIR               |
|      Beautiful brown leather      |
|        Excellent condition        |
|         £45, will deliver         |
|           Tel: 654326             |
+-----------------------------------+
```

Display

These adverts may be several columns wide, and may include pictures. Some publications now also offer semi-display adverts with a standard piece of artwork (bells for wedding congratulations, a stork for a new baby, etc.) at a special rate.

Wording

Before writing your advert, read a number of examples from the publication you have chosen. You will probably need to use some standard abbreviations (most adverts are paid for by the word or by the character, so it is economical to keep it as short as possible), and reading through a few published ads means you will become familiar with the jargon.

People rarely read adverts all the way through one after the other. There are far too many. Instead it is usual to skim the columns for catchwords. The first word or two of the advert are going to be the words that catch the eye of a potential buyer. They must therefore be accurate.

In a lineage advert never start with the words 'wanted' or 'for sale'. The classification should tell the reader that your item is for sale without you having to waste those important boldface words doing so. Instead, choose the word that your respondent will most likely be looking for – the name of the object or service wanted or offered, or the area of a flat or house to let or for sale:

Typing service, letters, thesis, manuscripts ...
Stereo equipment, tuner, amp, CD ...
Christmas trees, large, small ...
Tanning fast sunbeds ...
Kiswick house to let ...
Garage in Kiswick, central, secure ...

Apart from this, you will probably want to add as many details as you can. A lineage advert need not be grammatically correct.

Placing the advert

Placing classifieds is simply a matter of filling out the appropriate form. You will probably be asked to give the number or title of the classification you wish to use, and then to fill in the words in a series of single-word boxes.

Follow the rules for filling out other forms (see pp. 204-05). Make sure your writing is legible, or the copy-typist may make an error that renders your advert useless.

Writing lonely hearts adverts

These days, many people advertise for new friends and potential lovers through the classifieds. Not all do so because they are socially awkward. Many are busy people who have no time for the speculative social trawling necessary to find new friends in large cities, or who want to break out of a small circle of friends in search of new blood. This is especially the case with older people who may be divorced, widowed or separated.

Surveys have shown that the adverts in this classification that receive the most replies are those that say more about the advertiser and less about the kind of person they want to meet. Use this as a general rule of thumb, and you will have plenty of replies to choose from.

Again, read the lonely hearts column you want to use for ideas on how to present yourself. What you say will depend entirely on the kind of relationship you are looking for. Be truthful, especially when it comes to your physical appearance.

Responding to a lonely hearts ad

The main problem with responding to an advert of this sort is that your correspondent is anonymous, whereas you are compelled to give your phone number. You may decide to use a box number yourself, to avoid any unwelcome visits.

The letter you will write is a selling letter – you are selling yourself to the advertiser. You might like to give the following information:

- Your job, skills, qualifications.
- The area in which you live.
- Your marital status and nationality.
- A description of your character and maybe a reason for wanting to meet new people.
- Some of the things you enjoy doing. Be particular; if you enjoy reading, say what type of book, if you enjoy sports, say which sports and why.
- Close by suggesting the next step – a phone call or another letter, or even a meeting.

Don't feel you have to apologize for replying. Many people now use similar 'artificial' means of meeting new people, and so there should be no stigma attached. Any advertiser has already overcome the idea that advertising for friends is somehow socially defective, and you should too.

Use the best stationery you can afford, and if you are tempted to enclose a photograph, avoid using automatic passport photo machines. These never produce flattering results. If finding new friends is important to you, go to a professional photographer and have some studio shots taken.

A WORD OF WARNING

When arranging the first meeting, make sure you nominate a public place during reasonable hours to avoid getting into a 'difficult' situation with a stranger. Lunch is always a good idea.

COMPLAINTS

There are two basic rules for writing letters of complaint. The first is to leave yourself time to calm down (if you were initially angry about the incident) and the second is to consider whether you have a valid reason for complaining. Only make a complaint if you really are aggrieved, have been put at risk or seriously inconvenienced.

Most companies take customer complaints seriously, and run a Customer Relations department or something similar to answer questions and complaints. A telephone call will yield the name of the manager of that department.

Try to keep your letter courteous; avoid using an accusatory tone or demanding what is going to be done about it! Stating your case calmly and politely almost always brings a quick, positive response.

If you have used a product or service before and have never had cause to complain, say so. Your bargaining power is in your being a loyal customer who wishes to remain so, but may be turned away by the incident.

Dear Mrs Pickford

<u>X-Brand Baked Beans</u>
I spoke to your office today with regard to a piece of glass found in a 200 g can of X-Brand Baked Beans.

I bought the product from a local convenience store, and was shocked to find the glass inside the can as I emptied it into a saucepan.

I have used X-Brand Baked Beans for many years and have never had cause to complain before. However, the glass could have caused severe injury, and I would be glad to know that you are investigating the matter with your cannery.

I am enclosing both the glass and the base of the can bearing the product code. I hope to hear from you shortly.

Yours sincerely

As no damage was actually done, the letter is fairly gentle in tone. However, some complaints are more serious, and you may have good reason to word your letter of complaint more strongly.

Dear Mr Graves

This company has been using your delivery service for a number of years now, and until last May, we have never had cause for complaint.

However, since then, there have been several instances where deliveries have been late or the consignments have been wrong. This has been exacerbated by rudeness on the part of your staff, for which there can be no excuse.

As you know, we work to tight deadlines and cannot afford this kind of disruption. Please investigate this matter and let me know what action you propose to take. If there is no improvement in the service, we will need to consider seeking an alternative.

Yours sincerely

The above letter is a complaint and a warning. If the service is not improved, an alternative service will be sought. But what if the company fails to take note of the complaint?

Dear Mr Graves

I last wrote to you three weeks ago pointing out problems we were experiencing with your delivery service.

Despite your protestations and assurances, we are still having serious problems. The consignments have been late on two out of three occasions, and all have been missing important items.

It is clear that you are not willing or capable of improving your service to the standard we require and so I am terminating our relationship with your company.

Yours sincerely

Responding to letters of complaint

Letters of complaint should always be taken very seriously, especially if you are providing goods or services.

Your letter should be courteous, even if the complainant has abused you. You should be truthful – if you have already been having trouble with the product, say so. Try not to sound as if you are making excuses, but offer a reasonable explanation for the lapse. Never show that you do not believe the customer, or lead him to believe that the matter is not being taken seriously. Say that the customer's patronage is important to you, and apologize for inconvenience.

Dear Mr Lyle

Thank you for your letter of 15th June, regarding our delivery service. I am sorry that you are experiencing some problems, and have looked into the details of your account. I realize that you rely on our service for prompt delivery and am sorry that we have not been supplying a 100% service.

In May I set up a new packing team, and until they had settled in, there were some teething problems. However, the new staff are now fully trained, and I can assure you that there will be no repetition of the kind of problems you describe.

I apologize for the inconvenience to you, and assure you of our best attention at all times.

Yours sincerely

CONDOLENCE

However many chat-shows are devoted to discussing bereavement, and however many sympathetic articles and books published, most people will always find confronting death difficult beyond imagining. This is why letters of condolence are so difficult to write. It is hard to find the words that describe our feelings with sincerity and without cliché, because we are afraid most of all to mention death.

Drafting the letter

A letter as difficult as this will certainly need at least one, and perhaps two or three drafts. The point of a letter of condolence is to offer your support to the bereaved and to show that the dead person will be remembered in a positive light without writing a full obituary. To start the words flowing, think about the dead person, and jot down his or her outstanding qualities, remembering in particular your own relationship with them.

Some examples

The first example is to an older woman who has lost her husband after a long illness.

> Dear A_____,
> I was sorry to hear of G_____'s death. Even though he was ill for such a long time, it must still be a shock for you to find yourself without him.
> G_____ had many friends, and I was certainly not the closest of them, but I will miss his company, his awful jokes and that whiff of ready-rubbed tobacco that followed him everywhere.
> I know that your family are supporting you through this terrible time, but in the future, please feel that you can call on me for anything.
> My condolences once again,
> Sincerely,

The second example is to a man whose mother has been killed in a car accident.

> Dear A_____,
>   I was shocked to hear of your mother's death. You must have been devastated by the news. She was such a fit woman, we thought she would survive us all, and now there is a gap where she used to be. Your mother was one of the mainstays of this village, and we will miss her, as you will.
>   If you need some company in the weeks ahead, please consider my house open at any time of the day or night. If you need practical help with anything, you have only to ask.
>   My condolences, and my sympathy.
>   Sincerely,

The following letter is to a couple whose child has died in early infancy. This is happily a rare occurrence these days, but it is a situation that gives rise to what is probably the most difficult of these difficult letters. If death itself remains a taboo subject in this society, then the death of a child is even more unspeakable.

Avoid suggesting that the couple try for another baby immediately, and unless you have experienced a similar bereavement, do not say that you understand the parents' feelings.

> Dear A_____ and J_____,
>   I cannot imagine what you must have suffered in the past few weeks since C_____'s birth. It must be devastating to lose a child after such a struggle. You must be feeling bewildered with a confusion of emotions.
>   Please accept my deepest sympathy, and please feel that you can call me if you need any kind of help at all.
>   With love,

Editing for sincerity

When you have finished writing, it is worth checking the tone of the letter. It must have some real meaning for the person you are writing to, and must above all sound sincere. Edit out if you can any euphemisms; however hard it may be, use plain words. Erase any clichés; phrases that have been used frequently in less important situations and so have come to mean nothing: 'a great tragedy' is a prime example.

Do not shy away from speaking plain English (without saying anything hurtful or unkind). The most important point is to show that you understand the bereaved person's feelings, and even if that person sits down to weep over a particularly poignant memory your letter has evoked, tears are not necessarily a bad thing.

Finally, make sure that your letter is in keeping with your relationship to the bereaved. Be formal if you do not know them well; be intimate if you are a close friend or relative. Always handwrite a letter of this kind.

See also p. 258 on wording an announcement of death for a newspaper.

CONGRATULATIONS

There are many occasions on which it is appropriate to offer your congratulations: the passing of important exams; an engagement, marriage or birth; or a promotion at work. It is usual on all these occasions to confine the contents of your letter to just the subject in hand, keeping news, gossip or business for another letter. Here are some sentiments you might like to express on different occasions:

Passing exams

- Congratulations.
- Say how you heard the news.
- Name the exam.
- Mention the hard work that must have been done in study and revision.
- Ask questions about the future: will the student be going to a new job? will the student be continuing in education? will the new qualification help with promotion, or lead to a raise in salary?

> *Dear Edward,*
> *I heard from your father that you had passed your 'A'-levels with flying colours. Congratulations – you must have put in some very hard work to get such good grades. Will you be going on to university, or do you have a job lined up?*
> *Kind regards,*

Engagement

At one time it was not done to congratulate a woman on her engagement, only the man. However, with so many people setting up home together before they are married, our social code has become much less formal. Now it is acceptable to congratulate both the woman and the man, and even do it in a single letter addressed to them both.

- Congratulations.
- Say how you heard the news.
- Say how well you think the couple suit each other (if this is what you think).
- Ask when the wedding is expected to be.
- Ask to meet the 'other half' if you haven't already done so.
- Avoid mentioning previous relationships.

> *Dear Mary and Andrew,*
> *I spotted your names in the local newspaper last week, and thought I would drop you this note to offer my congratulations to you both. I'm sure everybody's saying it, but you really do make a wonderful couple, and I'm very happy that you have decided to tie the knot after so long together. Have you set a date yet?*
>
> *Kind regards,*

Marriage

- Congratulations.
- Say how you heard the news.
- Say what a good choice the couple have made.
- Wish the couple good luck for their new life together (even if they have been living together for a number of years, marriage is definitely a new step).
- Express your hope that the couple enjoys or enjoyed their honeymoon.
- As with engagements, avoid mentioning previous relationships.

> *Dear Mary and Andrew,*
> *Congratulations – you tied the knot at last! I was so glad to see your picture in the paper. You both looked very happy, and*

I hope that will continue.
 Good luck, and congratulations once again.
 Best regards,

Birth of a child

Keep your sentiments centred on mother and child and you won't go far wrong.

- Congratulations.
- Say how you heard the news.
- Wish mother and child well.
- Express your hope that they are both in good health.
- Ask questions: sex of the child; its weight; who does it look like; when will mother and child be home?

Dear Mary,
 Twins! Congratulations – a ready-made family. I hope you are all doing well, despite the shock, and that you will be going home soon.
 If Andrew needs any help while you are recovering and getting used to doing everything twice, let me know.
 Congratulations, once again.
 Best wishes,

Promotion

Congratulating a colleague, friend or business contact on a promotion or new job is a good way to stay in touch and foster goodwill. Avoid flattering your correspondent or criticizing his or her previous employers.

- Congratulations.
- Say how you heard of the move/promotion.
- Explain how you think the new job would suit the correspondent: new challenge; better location; better working conditions.

- Perhaps suggest a meeting/lunch/drinks.

Dear Helen

I read in the trade press that you have moved to a new job at Harris plc. Congratulations – I'm sure you will rise to the new challenges of a larger company, and that you will be very successful there.

Would you have time for lunch next week?

Best regards

Dear John,

I heard that you had landed that new job at Joiner Davis. Congratulations.

I hope you are settling in well. I'm sure this is the right move – you always wanted to work in the European market. Is Angela glad that you don't have to commute any more?

So good luck with the new job and congratulations once more.

Best regards,

COVER NOTES

A cover note is normally used when the sender wishes to transmit printed material (brochures, price lists, information packs, etc.), but has no other substantial message for the addressee. A covering *letter* is normally requested to accompany a CV in application for a job, and is usually more complex (see pp. 240-43)

A cover note is useful if you wish your addressee to have the impression that he or she has received a personal service, or if you wish to convey your name and position for the addressee's further use. The general rule is 'courteous but short'. You may wish to match the length of the message with the size of paper and use A5 rather than the standard A4.

> Dear Mr Blythe
>
> Thank you for your recent enquiry.
>
> I am enclosing our brochure, which should give you the details you require. If you have any other questions please call me on extension 278.
>
> Yours sincerely

With Compliments

If there is no need whatsoever to say anything to the addressee, then it may be appropriate to use a compliments slip instead of a cover note. See p. 17.

DISPUTES

Many disputes are conducted by letter, and perhaps the most familiar of all disputes are those with neighbours: the blaring radio, loud all-night parties (to which you are not invited, adding insult to injury), unsightly piles of scrap metal in the front garden, problems with fences, party walls, overgrown trees ... The catalogue is endless.

But most differences are solved quickly and easily with the right word in the right ear. Here are some guidelines:

- Wait until your temper has cooled before writing your letter.
- Use words of reason not a stream of obscenities.
- Explain your problem clearly and simply.
- Try to see the other person's point of view. Maybe it was causing a problem, perhaps some of this is your fault.
- Try to criticize not the person but the action.
- State clearly want you would like to be done.
- Remember the law, and don't say anything you are likely to regret.

All this does not mean you have to lie down and act the door-mat. If a first letter does not bring the desired response, you have every right to become more aggressive in your words, without descending to the level of insult or obscenity. Good humour often defuses a potentially explosive situation. On the other hand, a typed letter will alert the recipient to a serious matter at hand.

Dear Mr Bloggs

For the past few weeks now, my wife and I have been disturbed late at night by loud music being played in your garden shed.

I realize that the shed is quite a distance away from the house, but you must be using some pretty top-notch speakers, because we are being kept awake, and can hear most of the lyrics clearly.

I wonder if you would agree to turn the music down a little, say, after 10 p.m. We do go to bed quite early because I have to travel some distance to work each day. I would be most grateful if you would.

Yours sincerely

This letter is diplomatic. It flatters the neighbour by praising the quality of the speakers, but asks quite reasonably that the volume be turned down after a certain time. It should get a positive response. However, if it doesn't ...

Dear Mr Bloggs

I am sorry not to have received a response to my letter of 5th June, either in the form of a note, or a reduction in the noise pollution coming from your shed.

The disturbance is fast becoming intolerable, not least because you seem to have switched to a classical channel and I cannot bear opera after midnight.

Seriously, please attend to the matter or I may be forced to take action.

Yours sincerely

Again, there is a note of humour that takes the edge off the threat of action. At this stage, action need not be described, the threat should be enough to do the trick.

See also pp. 89-90 on bad language and abuse.

DIVORCE

The circumstances surrounding a divorce can vary widely. Some people are happy or relieved that they are free, while others feel lonely and rejected. So you may find yourself congratulating or commiserating with a newly divorced person. It is important to find out which is the case before putting pen to paper, but if you can't, it is best to err on the side of tea and sympathy. Avoid asking about the former wife/husband or voicing an expectancy that the new single will soon be part of a couple again.

Dear Alan,

David told me that your divorce has come through. The whole process must have been very distressing for you, and you have my sympathy. At least now, you can put the past behind you and make a fresh start with the support of some very loving friends.

If you feel like dropping round one weekend, you are always welcome.

Best regards,

Dear Catherine,

Congratulations. I heard your divorce finally came through. You must be feeling relieved that it is all over, but I know what a difficult time you must have been through.

Let's celebrate the single life with a night on the town soon.

Love,

FILLING IN FORMS

In today's society of information and classification, everybody is presented with forms to fill in: the census, voting papers, application forms for jobs, questionnaires, forms to join the local library, forms for bank loans, mortgages, insurance policies ... The list is endless.

Whether a form is short and simple, or long, complicated and of vital importance, the same guidelines apply:

- Read the form from start to finish before starting to fill it in. Instructions on how to fill in the form should be given at the top.
- Always use ink. Use a typewriter if you can. This is perhaps the best reason for retaining a typewriter in an office where word processors have taken over.
- Write using block capitals so that the information given is legible.
- Make sure you include documents asked for when returning the form.
- Make sure that you sign the form and add the date if requested to do so.
- Read the small print: you may be making a declaration where an error on your part could be construed as attempted fraud.

If the form is particularly important (applications for jobs, loans, etc.), then it is a good idea to make a photocopy and start by filling your answers in on that before copying them onto the original. This avoids mistakes on the real thing, enables you to fit everything you want to say into the space allotted, and can be retained as a useful copy for your own files.

See pp. 246-71 for information on filling in application forms for jobs.

Much of the information we pass on through forms is keyed into a computer database, and is therefore accessible to people we know nothing about. Through the Data Protection Act, it is possible to check information held in this way, and to ask that it is changed if it is incorrect. See p. 157 for information on the Data Protection Act.

FORM LETTERS

Form or standard letters are useful in offices where a large number of very similar letters are written every day. They may appear in several forms: pre-printed forms that list various options for the sender to communicate (see **Acknowledgments**); photocopied standard letters that are filled in with the relevant name and address; word-processed letters that are merged with a file of variables to produce what appear to be individually-produced letters.

See **Planning a Communication** pp. 48-9 for further details.

GET-WELL LETTERS

These days it is most common for people to send flowers to someone who is ill or in hospital, but even though flowers are a nice idea, a letter conveys your sympathy for a long time after the bouquets have wilted.

The most important thing is to put yourself in the position of the person who is sick. It may be possible gently to poke fun at a minor condition in which there is some pain, but no trauma. A patient with a very serious condition on the other hand would not be cheered by your making light of the situation, and so you should probably stick to sympathy and good wishes.

Here are some pointers:

- Start by saying how you heard of the person's illness (or if the source is not legitimate, i.e. you heard from local gossip, you might prefer to say simply that you heard).
- Commiserate and sympathize with the patient – try to imagine what it must be like to be in their position.
- Mention something that the patient might look forward to doing when they are well.
- Exhort the patient to 'get well soon', and assure them that they are in your thoughts.

Here is an example of a sister writing to her brother in a situation that is less than fatal.

> Dear Jack,
>   Annie tells me that they've finally managed to get you to go to hospital after all these years – and high time too.
>   Seriously, I'm sorry you are in pain and I hope your stay 'inside' won't be too harrowing. It will be worth it to get those toenails sorted out.
>   The grandchildren are waiting for their Sunday afternoon

> football referee to get back on his feet, so get well soon.
> *Stay cheerful. We're all thinking about you.*
> *Love,*

In this case, the sister is able to joke with her brother, but also to show her sympathy – while ingrowing toenails are not fatal, they are still painful. The reference to playing football is particularly appropriate to Jack's condition.

In the following example, the writer has realized that her friend is due for a long spell in bed, and that she may well suffer boredom. She also decides not to visit until Cathy is feeling up to seeing people.

> *Dear Cathy,*
> *I'm sorry to hear you've developed glandular fever. I understand it can be pretty nasty, quite apart from the boredom of having to stay in bed for weeks on end.*
> *I thought you might soon be feeling up to reading, so here are some magazines to keep you going.*
> *Get well soon, and when you're feeling better, I'll pop over to say hi. We miss you.*
> *Love,*

The two examples above are reasonably simple letters to put together. The most difficult of the Get-Well letters is to a person whose illness may be fatal. In this case it is necessary to strike a balance – extending sympathy without causing more anguish. You would not be thought a coward to use a card or flowers to convey your good wishes. Alternatively, you may find that you can express your feelings by writing to the sick person's husband, wife or other close relative; your sentiments will be passed on and you also have an opportunity to offer help to relatives who may also be in need of emotional or practical support.

Dear Colin,

I was so very sorry to hear about Jean's illness – it must have come as a great blow to both of you. Perhaps it is some small comfort to know that she is being treated in the best cancer hospital in the country.

I wanted you to know that you are in my thoughts and prayers. If there is anything I can do to help – shopping, babysitting, anything – please let me know.

Sincerely,

GOOD LUCK

As with letters of congratulation, wishing a person luck for a particular event is a good way to stay in touch and make your support known. There are a number of occasions on which you may feel it appropriate to wish a person good luck: examinations, a driving test or starting a new job.

For this kind of communication, it is nice to use a decorated card or postcard. Keep the message short and sweet and you cannot go wrong.

Examinations

Dear Paula,

I know you must be busy with last-minute revision, but I thought I would write to wish you all the best for your exams.

We all know how difficult the course has been for you – you certainly have worked very hard and deserve to pass with flying colours. Do let me know how you get on, and perhaps when the results come out we'll be getting together for a celebration.

Good luck.

With love,

Driving test

Dear Tim,

I heard that your driving test is scheduled for next week. Good luck, and watch out for those trees that have a nasty habit of jumping out when you're least expecting them ....

With love,

New job

Dear Caroline,

Andrew told me that you will be starting your new job next Monday. I hope your first day goes well – I'm sure you will be an instant hit. Good luck and best wishes for a successful future.

Kind regards,

INFORMATION

Many of the letters handled by the postal service each day are requests for information or contain information in response to such requests. It is in the interests of most businesses and bodies to give you the information you need, especially if you are considering buying something, and many bodies have departments whose sole purpose is to help you.

Requesting information

There are two keys to getting the right information: first is finding the person who can give you what you are looking for; second is making that person understand what it is you want to know.

Before you start, make sure that you know exactly what information it is you require, and consider who might best be able to give you that information.

Finding the right person

The route to finding the right person depends largely on the starting point. Most requests for information are to do with a company's goods or services. In this case, a phone call to the company's switchboard will enable you to discover that the company has a public relations, sales or marketing department, and you may even get a name.

Local government is a little more difficult, because it consists of many departments, often in several buildings. Your local library should have a booklet that lists the services that the local government provides, and give you a contact address. Alternatively, look in the telephone book under the name of your local government and then check with the office you have chosen that someone there will be qualified to answer your query. In the case of local government it is not always necessary to write to a particular person, but getting the right department is crucial. If you mail your query to the wrong department it may be a long time before it is forwarded to the relevant person for a reply.

You may be looking for information of another kind: facts and figures, perhaps, or you may be doing other research. In this case, you may need specialist information from institutions or other public bodies. Whitaker's *Almanack* is indispensable in this situation, because it gives a list of most of the national societies, institutions and charities in the country. You will probably find it in the reference section of your local library. A phone call or letter to one of these may well put you on the trail of the expert who can help. Alternatively, the Registrar's Office at a university may be able to put you in touch with a member of staff working in your field.

The Registrar is also the person to write to if you are seeking information about courses offered by a college or university.

Asking the right questions

Extracting useful information from somebody is a matter of asking the right questions. On one hand, the procedure may be very simple: you may wish to receive information on a company's product. On the other hand, you may have a list of queries each involving a whole train of thought.

The best way to go about more complex queries is to make a list of all the information you need. When you draft your letter, you may like to give a brief indication of why you want the information, and then simply list the questions in order of importance. Remember to cut out any irrelevant information – anything that the addressee does not need to know. Stick to only those facts that will enable the person to understand what you are trying to find out:

Dear Sir

I have recently bought the house at the above address and would like to modernize it.

I would be very grateful if you would let me know whether I am eligible for a grant to cover some of the cost of the work, and how I go about applying.

Yours faithfully

The above letter requesting information about a house renovation grant contains enough information for the addressee to send a pre-printed booklet describing the eligibility criteria and the procedure for applying for the grant. The address is to be found in information from the local library, or from the telephone book.

This letter can be used as a standard when requesting information that is likely to be pre-printed for sending out on request (brochures, prospectuses, company annual reports, application forms and instructions, etc.). It involves a short explanatory sentence, then a paragraph outlining the information required. The following letter is based on the one above, but requests information about a product seen in an advertisement:

Dear Sir

I read about your new personalized date-stamping system in yesterday's *Daily News*.

I would be grateful if you would send me further information including: unit cost; discount for bulk buying; delivery periods and payment terms.

Yours faithfully

This correspondent has begun the letter with a sentence that explains where she saw the product advertised. This information is not necessary for the request, but makes the letter sound less abrupt. She would like any product information that is available, but also has three specific queries. Adding them to the letter at this stage means that she will receive all the information she requires, rather than a pre-printed package that may not include answers to her specific questions.

Responding to requests for information

Requests for information can take up a great deal of office time, so it is a good idea to try to anticipate the kinds of requests your company is likely to receive, and draw up a standard letter or produce an information sheet or brochure, which can be sent out with a compliments slip. See pp. 48-9 on standard letters.

It is especially important to be armed with materials of this kind if you are advertising a product or service, so that you are not caught off-guard by the rush of enquiries.

Even if you are prepared with a standard letter and pre-printed information, always read the letter of enquiry carefully, and ensure that you send all the information required. If you don't you may find a second or even a third letter landing on your desk asking for clarification or further information which could easily have been sent out the first time round. The advantage to the company is clear – you will save a great deal of time and energy in unnecessary correspondence. But if you are trying to sell a product, the advantages of a quick, complete response are even greater: you are likely to make the sale promptly rather than risking your potential buyer losing interest as the weeks go by.

If you need to write a covering letter, make sure you are courteous and business-like.

The following letter responds to the enquiry about date-stamping systems.

Dear Mrs Broad

Thank you for your enquiry about our new date-stamping system. I am enclosing our brochure, which gives general information about the product.

In answer to your specific queries:

1 Unit cost is £5.50 + VAT at 17.5%
2 We offer a discount of 10% on orders of 20 units or more
3 We will be able to deliver your order within ten days of receiving it.
4 Unless you already have an account with us, we will require payment with your order.

If you have any further questions, please give me a call.

Yours sincerely

The opening paragraph is friendly and courteous, and refers to the enclosure. As a general rule, always mention enclosures in the body of your letter, and indicate after the signatory that they are present using the letters Enc(s).

The correspondent has used a series of numbered points to answer each of the enquirer's questions in turn. Instead of numbers, you could use 'bullet points' (●) or asterisks (*). This layout makes the information immediately clear, and avoids the need to write complete sentences. The list method can also be used if, in asking for information, you have a number of quite detailed specific questions.

The correspondent has answered the questions in the order that they were given, for clarity.

See also pp. 299-302 for requesting information from a bank.

INSURANCE

Almost everyone finds it necessary to take out an insurance policy, either on a car, on house contents or on a single item of special value. Most people now make first contact with insurance companies by telephone, requesting information, but doing so by letter enables you to state exactly the kind of arrangement you are looking for to avoid wasting time with unsuitable policies.

Before you start to write, consider the items you want to insure, their value and the amount of compensation you would like should anything happen to them. Consider also the security arrangements you have made for their safe-keeping. When insuring possessions and house contents, most insurance companies also take into consideration the area in which you live and the size of your household.

> Dear Sir
>
> I have just moved to a new house at the above address and would like to take out contents insurance.
>
> I would like a policy that covers fire, flood and theft, and that covers items of value when they are taken out of the house. No single item is worth more than £1,500, and I would wish to be compensated 'old for new' in the event of a claim.
>
> The house has three bedrooms, and I live there together with my husband and a single child of eight years old. All doors and windows are secured with locks, and the house is fitted with a burglar alarm.
>
> Please would you send me details of a policy that would provide me with the kind of cover I require, and a quotation.
>
> Yours sincerely

If the worst happens, and you need to make a claim against an insurance policy, it is necessary to do so quickly and accurately so that the required compensation arrives soon enough to do some good.

To make a claim effectively, it must state all the facts and it must be accompanied by all the necessary documentation. Check that your facts are really accurate. Any mistakes you make could lead to charges of fraud. Read carefully the insurer's instructions to claimants and follow them. You may need to make a phone call to the insurer's office to find out exactly what is needed.

The letter should be laid out as a business letter. The subject line should be the number of your policy.

> Dear Sir
>
> Claim on Policy HC204/36789LB/0987
> I would like to make a claim under the house contents policy above, for the value of items stolen during a burglary at my house on the night of Monday 26th May 1994.
>
> I am enclosing the police crime report, and a list of the items that are missing, including their makes, serial numbers and replacement value. Further to this, I am sending you photographs of my wife's jewellery, which was also stolen.
>
> I would be glad if you would acknowledge receipt of this claim and process it as quickly as possible.
>
> Yours faithfully

It would be irrelevant to tell the insurance clerk that you came home last night, all wet and cold, after driving from the city where you were conducting business, to find that your house had been broken into (the intruders had obviously entered through a downstairs window) and many items stolen, including your wife's diamond eternity ring, which you gave her only two years ago, the stereo with its new CD player and the top-of-the-range TV.

Instead, do as the writer of the sample letter does: use the letter to convey the barest of the facts and allow the enclosures to tell the rest of the story. Never send documents as important as the ones mentioned in this letter through the post without taking copies of them first.

INVITATIONS

Receiving and replying to invitations were once a fixed part of most people's social life. At one time, even invitations to visit someone at home were printed and formally addressed. With the advent of the telephone and less formality in social life, many invitations are extended by word of mouth, and responses are acceptable in the same manner. Formal invitations are now only used on very special occasions, such as weddings, special wedding anniversaries, coming-of-age parties, etc., and informal invitations written as short letters are much more common.

This section starts with formal invitations, and goes on to discuss other types of invitation and replies to them. See pp. 313-15 for examples of wording for wedding invitations.

Formal written invitations

Formal invitations are normally printed on cards and include standard wording:

Mr & Mrs R. Baines
request the pleasure of the company of
Andrew Lloyd
on the occasion of the 21st Birthday
of their son,
Charles
at Holywell House Hotel, Juniper Lane
Holywell
on
Friday, 18th June 1994

RSVP   7.30 p.m.
Holywell Lodge   Lounge suit
Holywell   Carriages 12.30
(0098) 654321

This formal invitation to a 21st birthday party is extended by the birthday boy's parents. It gives all relevant details, including starting time and dress. A telephone number has been given, so replies can be made over the telephone. The absence of a telephone number indicates that you should respond in writing.

The word 'Carriages ...' indicates the time the function is expected to end.

What to wear

Many invitations include a note on what kind of thing to wear, but often that note is cryptic. Here is the key to solving the riddle:

Code	Men	Women
White tie	full evening dress: white tie, tails, wing collar, etc.	ball gowns and jewels
Black tie	dinner jacket/bow tie	evening wear (long or short dresses, skirts or evening trousers)
Lounge suit	smart business suit	business suits or cocktail dresses

At Home cards

These are used when inviting people to an event at one's own home: drinks, cocktails, dinner, etc. When invitations are to the home, it is usually the woman of the house who issues the invitation. The guests' names are handwritten at the top left-hand corner of the card.

Mr & Mrs G Dobson

Mrs Andrew Price
At Home
on Friday, 26th August

RSVP   Drinks
78 Cornwell Gardens   7–9 p.m.
Cornwell CL1 7TG

Responding to a formal invitation

Responses to formal invitations are usually written on post-cards or personalized cards. The response should be phrased in the third person, just as the invitation is phrased in the third person:

Andrew Lloyd would like to thank
Mr & Mrs R. Baines for their kind invitation to celebrate
Charles's 21st Birthday at Holywell House Hotel on 18th June, and
is pleased to accept.

If you have to turn down an invitation, it is polite to give a good reason.

Andrew Lloyd would like to thank
Mr & Mrs R. Baines for their kind invitation to celebrate
Charles's 21st Birthday at Holywell House Hotel
on 18th June, but regrets that he is unable to accept because of a
prior engagement.

ROYAL INVITATIONS
The most formal of all invitations are, of course, those extended by Royalty. Invitations from the Monarch, are usually considered to be commands rather than requests, and so your reply should use the word 'obey', rather than 'accept'.

Informal invitations

Even if you love to use the telephone, an informal written invitation acts as an *aide-mémoire* to the recipient. It can be laid out in the same way as one would lay out any other personal letter. It should be handwritten.

The invitation

An informal invitation should include most if not all of the information given in a formal invitation:

- Type of event (dinner, drinks, etc.).
- Day and date, time, venue.
- Other guests if the event is intimate.
- Dress.

Be sure to:

- Be clear about who you are inviting. You may be writing to one person, but may wish to include a spouse or friend.
- Give your address and telephone number.
- Give directions unless you are sure your guests know the way.

Dear Angie,

Nick and I have finally succeeded in bringing order to the new house, and we were wondering whether you and Bob would be free for a celebration dinner here on Friday 15th April. You'll be relieved to hear that Nick will be on duty in the kitchen rather than me.

We've also asked Jane and Chris, and Andrea has promised to bring her new man, the mysterious Russian.

We're aiming to eat at around 8.30 p.m., so we'll be ready for you at around 7.30. Dress is casual, as always. Do let me know if you can make it – it would be wonderful to see you both after so long.

Kind regards,

The response – accepting

Include the following:

- Thanks for the invitation.
- Name the event.
- Say you can attend and how nice it will be.
- Any other information.
- Say you look forward to the occasion.

Dear Sally,

Thank you for your invitation. Bob and I would love to come on the 15th. It will be nice to see Jane, Chris and Andrea and, of course, your new home.

Bob is working out of town that day, so we probably won't get to you until about 8 p.m., if that's all right.

We look forward to seeing you then.

Best regards,

The response – declining

Include the following elements:

- Thanks for the invitation.

- Positive sentiment about wanting to come.
- Identify the event.
- Give reason for declining.
- Apologies and plans to meet, where appropriate.

> *Dear Sally,*
> *Thanks for your invitation. We would love to come on the 15th, but we're celebrating our anniversary that weekend, and Bob has already booked a trip to Paris.*
> *I'm sorry we won't be able to make it. If my memory serves me right, it will be a great shame to miss Nick's culinary delights.*
> *We must plan to meet. It really has been too long since we saw you both, so let's set a date soon. In the meantime, have a great time on the 15th.*
> *Kind regards,*

Invitation to a children's party

Shop-bought children's party invitations often come with a reply slip attached, which can be very handy. Alternatively, if your child is old enough, he or she could have fun creating their own party invitations. Check them for the information content. Here is an example:

Susan Sheen
is invited to
Andrew Morgan's
Fancy Dress Birthday Party
at
4–6 p.m. on
Thursday 26th April 1995
56 Grove Walk
Huntston
RSVP 2620473

Invitation to stay

Dear Jill and Bob,

   Thank you for your house-warming card. Now that we've settled in we were wondering whether you would like to try out the spare bed over Easter.

   Mum and Dad are coming on Easter Sunday, so it would be a good opportunity to catch up on family gossip. On Easter Monday we were thinking of a visit to Angler Bay. How about turning up on Saturday afternoon?

   I've already made the bed up so you can't say no! Give me a call.

                                    Love,

UNINVITED GUESTS

Sometimes a person may be tempted to bring a friend to a function to which they alone have been invited. To avoid embarrassment on the part of the host and the guest, make it a practice to ask your host first.

JOB APPLICATIONS

Some of the most important letters any person has to write are letters of application for a job. Only a generation ago, the majority of the workforce began work as teenagers or young adults and continued with the same company until they retired some 45 years or so later. These people may never have drafted a curriculum vitae (CV) or a written application for a job.

However, the job market has changed a great deal in recent years. School-leavers no longer move automatically into apprenticeships, vocational training courses or further education. Young adults find that they cannot wait ten years for promotion within their starting company, and so need to look for new challenges elsewhere. People in their forties and fifties are increasingly thrown on to a job market through redundancy. The whole spectrum of the workforce is now highly mobile and so finding a job has never been a more competitive business.

This means that the people dealing with job applications are often snowed under, and they will never be able to interview everyone who applies. They will have a few criteria by which to choose a small number of people, and those are the people who have submitted a faultless CV and covering letter, who have some idea what the job and the company are about, and can present themselves in the best possible light.

Types of application

Jobs are either advertised in the press, made known by word of mouth or found by 'speculative application' (writing to a company that has not advertised but may by chance need your services).

If responding to an advert, you will often find that the

advertiser has specified the means of application. Advertisers may:

- Request a handwritten letter of application.
- Request a Curriculum Vitae (in which case always include a covering letter).
- Give an address or telephone number for requests for an application form.

If the job has not been advertised, you will need to send a covering letter and a CV.

So there are three documents that need to be dealt with: CVs, letters of application and application forms.

Putting together a CV

'Curriculum vitae' means 'the road of life'. It gives a picture of your career and some other personal details. CVs should be short and informative: one or two sides is just right. More than this is too much. A CV cannot be compiled quickly. It requires a great deal of thought, and possibly three or four redrafts, checking facts, wording, spellings and grammar, and taking care over layout.

Many people find it useful to consult a bureau that will draft and type a CV using the information you give them on a questionnaire. Such bureaux should be employing experts in recruitment, rather than a pool of typists, and it is important that you meet a consultant personally rather than doing it all by post. A good bureau is expensive, and a bad bureau is not worth consulting. Try to get as much information as possible before committing yourself.

Planning

A CV can be broken down into a number of sections. Each section requires certain information to be given (the listed order is recommended):

Personal details

- Full name.
- Contact address in full.
- Contact telephone number.
- Date of birth and age.
- Marital status and details of children, if any.
- Nationality (immigration status).

Statement of objectives

A short paragraph stating your purpose; e.g. to secure a position giving greater responsibility, more flexibility, new challenges, in which to exercise skills already obtained.

Education

List in chronological order:

- Names and addresses of schools at secondary level.
- Dates attended.
- Secondary qualifications.
- Names and addresses of colleges or universities.
- Dates attended.
- Qualifications obtained.

Training courses

List in chronological order:

- Names of courses and duration (do not list courses of less than a week).
- Dates attended.
- Qualifications (if appropriate).

Other skills

- Fluency or working knowledge of languages.
- Driving licence.
- Computer software/language skills, etc.

Employment

List in chronological order (or alternatively in reverse chronological order, giving the last position first):

- Dates of employment.
- Name and address of employers.
- Employer's business if not obvious.
- Your position.
- Short description of responsibilities, number of staff supervised, any particular successes, reason for leaving.

Personal interests

List activities genuinely pursued: voluntary work; playing a musical instrument; reading a certain type of book; involvement with a certain sport; a certain form of cooking, art, performance arts, etc.

Referees

Either give names and addresses of people who have agreed to act as referees, or indicate that references are available on request. It is polite to contact potential referees before submitting their names and ask for permission to do so. (Sample letters on this subject are to be found on pp. 273-4.)

The right information

The amount of information that you include in a CV, and how that information is balanced, depends on how far down the road of life you have come. If you are a school-leaver with only Saturday jobs and vacation work on the list, then you will devote more space to your education, listing in full your grades, and detailing positions of responsibility and other school honours. It would be very odd, on the other hand, if you are a 35-year-old salesman with twelve years of work behind you to still be listing that you were house captain and won the county debating contest at the age of 16.

The general rule is to give more space and detail to recent events. For example, if you have 'O'-levels, 'A'-levels and a degree, list the number of secondary qualifications only, but give full details of the degree. If you have had two jobs since leaving school, give more space to those and less space to Saturday or vacation work. If you are established at a high level in your industry or business, you may omit details of secondary education altogether and simply list your further education. If you stand on a road and look back the way you have come, perspective makes objects in the far distance smaller, and it is not possible to see so much detail. In the same way, it is desirable to draw a picture of your career that gives a clear vista but more detail in the foreground.

Ironing out problems

A CV is intended as an outline only, but it will probably also be used by the employer as a starting point for questions in the interview, so when making an initial list of items you wish to include, consider how they may provoke questions, and how you might react to them.

It may be that there are items that you do not wish to include on your CV. This is most often a mistake. Gaps in the chronological order of your life will be noticed, and if you get to the interview stage, you will be asked what happened in that time. Unemployment is no longer the stigma that it used to be, and most employers even expect periods of unemployment.

However, if you can say you were active during that time (worked as a volunteer, brushed up on your French, took evening classes, devoted your time to bringing up children), then this will be a plus for you. The longer your unemployment, the more you will need to fill it in terms of serious activities.

You may also come up against the problem of how to deal with having been given the sack. No-one wants to employ a serious troublemaker or 'difficult' co-worker, so you will need to find words that prevent the alarm bells ringing. In extreme cases, in which you may have been fired, you may wish to omit this fact altogether. In which case, omit your reasons for leaving in every other case. It is more likely, however, that you were asked to resign, or simply made redundant. If you were asked to resign, you may state 'resigned position in order to seek more challenging appointment/greater responsibility/a position in a smaller company'. Make sure your wording is *active*, and try to show how your resignation has been advantageous.

If you have been made redundant, remember that it is positions and functions that are redundant rather than people. Your company may have been contracting due to the pressures of a contracting market, or they may have decided to consolidate in an aspect of their business that did not involve your function, e.g. ' Made redundant when the company decided to concentrate its efforts in distribution rather than manufacture due to sharp increases in operating cost'. This formula shows that you have a knowledge of your company's decision-making processes and a realistic view of the marketplace.

In both cases it is not a good idea to seem bitter. The CV is not the place to air grievances, to snipe at former employers or to crow over them. For one thing, the prospective future employer may be in contact with your former company, and may even do business with them.

Beware, be honest, be positive.

The right words

Most advertisers receive large numbers of CVs, and if they are all perfectly typed and laid out, the only way you are going to make an impact is if you use words that grab attention. These are not the kinds of words used in banner headlines, just words that show you are energetic, enthusiastic and knowledgeable in your field.

Active words

Most employers want to find people who are active and energetic, even if they do not say as much in their advertisements. Therefore, avoid passive constructions: 'I took responsibility for' is better than 'I was involved in', 'I managed' is better than 'I was asked to deal with.' Here are some other active constructions:

- I developed
- I created
- I took responsibility for
- I managed
- I devised
- I controlled
- I initiated
- I responded to
- I negotiated

Simple words

Using simple words is not a mark of simple-mindedness. Short, well-chosen words ensure clarity. Long words often give the impression of pomposity, and even stupidity, when they are used incorrectly. It is always possible to find a phrase to cover the meaning of a more difficult term, and it is desirable that you do this whenever possible.

Jargon

If you must use technical terms and jargon, make sure that you are using them correctly, and that you include terms that are widely used in your field. Unless they really are in the mainstream, avoid using abbreviations: computer-aided design is better than CAD, but RSPCA or BBC are acceptable. If your prospective employer is not directly involved in your field, be especially careful. A person who was once a state-registered nurse, but has since retrained and is now applying for a job in computing, may decide to write SRN as 'State-registered nurse (SRN)'.

First person singular

Even in a CV – the only document dedicated to talking about oneself – using the first person can become wearing to the reader. Some people avoid this by adopting a telegraphic style: 'I managed a team of five' becomes 'Managed a team of five', for example. Others write their CVs in the third person, so that 'I managed a team of five' becomes 'She managed a team of five'. The first solution is, however, more widely used. Whichever solution you opt for, make sure that you use that form of words throughout, and avoid switching from 'I managed', to 'Managed' to 'She managed', which is just hopelessly confusing.

Checking your English

Never send out a finished CV unless it has been read by at least one person other than yourself. However good your spelling may be, there may be one error that you simply did not see, and that one error could cost you an interview.

For further notes on good written English, see **Planning a Communication** and **Punctuation and Spelling** .

Presentation and layout

Most CVs are laid out in a similar way, giving information in a certain order. The following sample CVs are laid out in a variety of ways, and all are acceptable because they enable the reader to find the information fast.

The first belongs to a school-leaver with a very limited employment record.

Curriculum Vitae

Name:	Damien Halliday
Address:	26 Farmer's Court
	Oxleigh
	OX3 8TB
Tel:	Oxleigh 6548765
Date of birth:	1.1.77
Age:	16
Marital status:	Single
Nationality:	British

Objective
To secure an entry-level position in electrical engineering that combines vocational training, direct shop-floor experience and good promotion prospects.

Education
1990–1994   Oxleigh Comprehensive, School Street, Oxleigh
Qualifications: 8 GCSEs: English, Mathematics, Design and Technology, Physics, Chemistry, Geography, History, German.

Other Skills
Working knowledge of German
Basic keyboard skills

Employment
1993–present Goodfood Hamburgers Ltd, High Street, Oxleigh
Superior: Mr H. Ashton, Manager
Position: Counter assistant
Weekend job taking food orders and serving customers. Won
Assistant-of-the-Month award for three months running.

Personal interests
Reading science fiction. Maintaining and using home
computer system. Member of Oxleigh Under-18 Football Club.

The second CV is that of a woman returning to work after her
children have left school. She has laid special emphasis on her
activities while a full-time mother, and has mentioned in particular
those that show she has administrative skills. This
example shows how to head the second page of the CV.

CURRICULUM VITAE

Maureen Alison Hendrix
26 The Close
Oxleigh OX4 6FD
0043–6019876

Date of Birth:	15/7/50	**Status:**	Married
Age:	43	**Children:**	Two children
Nationality:	British		at university

OBJECTIVE

To secure a part-time position that offers a variety of tasks, in
which to put to good use my organizational and secretarial
skills.

EDUCATION

Dates: **1961–1966**
School: Oxleigh High Scool for Girls, Albany
                                   Road, Oxleigh
Qualifications: Eight 'O'-Levels including English and
                                   Mathematics.

Dates: **1966–1968**
College: Oxleigh Secretarial College, College
                                   Road, Oxleigh
Qualifications: Shorthand Grade 2; Typing Grade 3.

Dates: **1992–1993**
College: Oxleigh Secretarial College, College
                                   Road, Oxleigh
Qualifications: Secretarial Skills Refresher Course:
                                   Shorthand (100 w.p.m.);
                                   Typing (60 w.p.m.).
                                   Book-keeping Grade One.
                                   Word processing.

CURRICULUM VITAE

Maureen Alison Hendrix

–2–

EMPLOYMENT

Date: **1968–1970**
Company: Oxleigh Light Industries Ltd.
Position: Secretary to the sales manager.
Responsibilities: Taking shorthand, typing and filing

correspondence, maintaining diaries, office support, etc.

Reason for leaving: Arrival of my first child.

OTHER SKILLS AND OCCUPATIONS

I was an active member of Oxleigh School PTA for eight years, including two years as secretary. I now work regularly as a volunteer for Help the Aged, which includes co-ordinating fundraising events. I also have a clean driver's licence and a good working knowledge of French. My personal interests include dressmaking and writing letters (I have a French penfriend of long standing).

References Available On Request

The third sample CV belongs to a graduate who is looking for his third full-time job. Notice how he stresses not only his responsibilities in his previous jobs, but is also able to quantify his performance.

CURRICULUM VITAE

Name: Gerald Matthew Rowbottom
Address: 198 Ramsey Row
                     Eppingham, EM12 3PL
Telephone: Home: Eppingham 6548721
                     Work: 071-000-8765 (direct line)
Date of birth: 20.2.63
Age: 30
Marital status: Single
Nationality: British

OBJECTIVE   To secure a sales position leading in due course to management. To widen my knowledge of the European market for educational books and utilize my language skills.

EDUCATION AND TRAINING

1976–1982	**Eppingham Boys Grammar School, Eppingham**
	Ten 'O'-levels, three 'A'-levels (French, German, English)
1983–1986	**Sanderswell University**
	BA (Hons) Modern Languages 2.1
July 1987	**Forum Business College, London**
	'Make that Deal!' one-week sales training course (residential)

EMPLOYMENT

1979–1985
Part-time and vacation work including book shop assistant and bar manager.

1986–1989   **Edward Blake & Sons, Trade Publishers**

Position: Travelling sales representative for the north west region.

Manager: John Blake, Sales Director

Responsibilities: Maintaining sales with existing bookshops; finding potential new customers.

Successes: Increased sales in the region by 35% in the first two years, and by a steady 10% in successive years. Successfully introduced the company's list of reference titles to non-traditional outlets such as stationery retailers.

1989–1994   **Books for Education Ltd, Education Publishers**

Position: Joined the company as sales representative for London, and was transferred in 1991 to the Africa sales team.

Manager: Anna Brightwell, Manager Overseas Sales

Responsibilities: As an active member of the Africa team, I negotiated the sale of books to clients in Anglophone and Francophone African countries.

Successes: Increased the sales of text books to Nigeria by 15%, reduced costs by finding alternative transportation suppliers. Instrumental in the forging of a major contract with the largest distributor in Cameroon.

OTHER SKILLS AND EXPERIENCE

One year (1982–1983) spent travelling in France and Germany, including work as a holiday campsite attendant. I speak fluent French and German. I have a clean driver's licence and Advanced Driver's Certificate, along with a full British passport.

PERSONAL INTERESTS

Reading contemporary fiction. Independent travel. Visual arts. Modern jazz. Squash and swimming.

REFERENCES

References are available on request.

KEY POINTS: NOTES FOR GOOD PRESENTATION

- Use headings for each section
- Use headings for each job or school
- Type headings in a consistent style: underlined, capitals, bold, etc.
- If you have the option, use as few typefaces as possible
- Select a typeface that is easy to read
- Use good quality white A4 paper and matching envelopes
- Never use personalized stationery or letterhead
- Type on one side only
- Use a typewriter that gives clear letters, and fit a new ribbon if necessary
- Do not use a typewriter that types some letters askew
- Never present a CV that has liquid paper corrections
- Leave good margins at the sides and at the foot of the page

Covering letters

All CVs should be accompanied by a covering letter. This should tell the employer which job you are applying for and a few words drawing attention to salient parts of your CV, saying why you are interested in the job, and why you think you would be suitable for the job. Your covering letter is a very important part of the application, and so it will require a great deal of thought.

Planning a covering letter

Read the advertisement *carefully*. Find out as much as you can about the company advertising the job by telephoning for a copy of their Annual Report (if it is a public company) or asking around. Put yourself in the shoes of the advertiser, and try to get an all-round picture of the person they are looking for.

All job advertisements are worded to attract a certain type of person. Apart from telling you what qualifications you need to have, the advertiser will use words that describe the kind of personality they wish to employ. They may use some of the following phrases:

- self-starter
- with initiative
- looking for a challenge
- working knowledge of
- experienced
- outgoing personality
- keep a cool head
- flexible
- mature
- self-motivated
- ambitious
- articulate.

Next, look through your CV and decide which points prove that you have the background and qualifications necessary. You will need to draw attention to these items in the letter.

Finally, it may be that you lack one or more of the skills or attributes asked for. If it seems to you that you could do the job despite this lack, you will need to say so in the letter. You may have some parallel or similar experience that you can point to as a substitute.

Retail Manager
Privately-owned accessories retailer requires self-starter to open and run small town-centre boutique. Working initially with one assistant, you will be responsible for buying, display and

re-orders and book-keeping. Managerial experience essential, with five years in retailing, preferably in accessories. CV and indication of salary requirements to: Jean Baird, Pretty Lady Ltd, 46 Beech Grove, Siltwell SL5 8UJ.

> *Dear Ms Baird,*
>
> *Retail Manager*
> *I am interested in applying for the position of Retail Manager advertised in yesterday's Evening Post.*
>
> *As you will see from my CV, which is enclosed, I have been working in retail for nine years, for most of that time in ladies' fashions. My current position is Assistant Manager at a store that includes a range of accessories, for which I am solely responsible. While I have not held the position of Manager, I have stepped in as acting manager on a number of occasions. My previous jobs have all involved book-keeping, dealing with wholesalers and window-dressing.*
>
> *Opening a new shop is an exciting prospect that requires hard work, and I would welcome the opportunity to build on my past experience to make the venture a success.*
>
> *I would be glad to meet you to discuss the position at your convenience. I would be grateful, however, if for the time being you would contact me at home rather than at work. I look forward to hearing from you.*
>
> *Your sincerely,*
>
> *Susan Moore (Miss)*
> *Enc.*

In this example, Susan Moore has noted all the points requested in the advertisement. She shows enthusiasm for the venture and has clearly thought about what the job is likely to entail. She has avoided platitudes about working with the public and enjoying wearing or buying fashion accessories, which are irrelevant.

The most important thing about this letter, though, is that she has confronted the main problem with her application and tried to find a solution: she does not have direct managerial experience. However, she has indicated that she has acted as manager in her own manager's absence, and this may be enough to get her an interview. She has also requested that she is contacted at home rather than at work, probably because she has not yet informed her present employers that she is looking for a new job.

As with the example opposite, try to keep the covering letter to one side; four or five paragraphs should be enough to introduce yourself and make an impression. Note that this covering letter has been handwritten, in fully-blocked style.

WRITTEN OR TYPED?

Most employers like to see a handwritten covering letter. Many will ask for this in advertisements. However, if there is not a specific instruction to do so, and your handwriting leaves something to be desired, perhaps it might be wise to type your letter, and there is nothing to stop you doing this. CVs, on the other hand should *always* be typed.

Speculative letters

One way to get around the intense competition in today's job market is to write to possible employers in the hope that they can find a place for you. While the chances of securing an interview are not high, you may at least secure a place in the personnel files, and may be considered for interview when the next suitable opening appears.

Some preliminary research will be necessary to find the companies that definitely employ people with your skills and background. Libraries hold directories of companies, which will give details of their business. Asking friends and family may also bring useful information.

When you have the information you need, draft your letter with the following points in mind:

- What has prompted you to choose this company in particular? It may run training courses or it may be expanding into your field, for instance.
- What kind of job are you looking for?
- What skills do you have to offer?

In the case of the speculative letter it is your aim to make the addressee turn the page and read your CV, and after that, to invite you to the company's offices for a 'discussion'. Sound enthusiastic about the company and flexible in terms of the role you might be able to play, and the company is more likely to be able to find a job for you.

Here is an example:

Dear Mr Penney

I understand that CBA Industrial runs a training scheme for school-leavers interested in pursuing a career in electrical engineering. I am currently a pupil at Digby Comprehensive. I will be leaving school this summer, and have decided to enter this field.

I am taking GCSEs in seven subjects, and have always done well in sciences, so expect to pass those subjects in the examinations this summer. I believe that it is important to learn while gaining work experience, and this is why I would like to opt for an apprenticeship scheme rather than further education. CBA Industrial is a large company, and I hope that this would enable me to gain experience in a number of different jobs before I am asked to specialize.

If you have time, I would be very interested to talk to you about possible work or training in this field. Perhaps I could pay you a visit late one afternoon after school finishes, or during the half-term break next month? I am enclosing my CV for your information.

Yours sincerely

Peter Brown
Enc.

Peter Brown has obviously done some research into the company's training programme (and he has also found out the name of the personnel officer), and this means he can say why he would like to join the company and why the company should employ him. He makes it clear at the end of the letter that he would like to meet the personnel officer – not for an interview, but simply to discuss possibilities. It should get a favourable response, if not a place on the programme.

Here is another example, from someone a little further along the career path.

Dear Mrs Gray

I read in the trade press over the weekend that Addington Advertising is about to attack the European market. I am looking for a new challenge in my career as an advertising account executive, with the possibility of a managerial role, and wondered whether you might be looking to employ extra staff to spearhead this move.

As you will see from the enclosed CV, I am Anglo-French with an unbroken track record in servicing existing clients and securing new accounts. My previous employers include companies in both England and France and I have acquired an in-depth knowledge of the advertising industry in both countries. I have family and friends in both London and Paris and so I would happily travel between the two countries, or even relocate to France if necessary.

I have been watching with interest Addington's expansion over the past few years and I have admired the company's work on a number of occasions. With this new step on the company's part, this seems an ideal time to contact you.

If you think I may be of service, I would be extremely interested to discuss the possibility of my joining you. I look forward to hearing from you.

Yours sincerely
Jean-Claude Alderman
Encs

With his cross-Channel experience and his language abilities, it seems that if the company is indeed looking for new staff, Jean-Claude Alderman would be a prime candidate. Any employer would be impressed and flattered by his knowledge of the company's successes and aspirations.

Application forms

Many companies make use of standard application forms, and ask applicants to telephone or write for a form, which must then be submitted by a certain date. The standard application form usually covers all the items in a standard CV, but may also include questions about your general health and more wide-ranging 'essay-style' questions about the kind of job you are looking for, what characteristics you have that may make you suitable for the job and questions about your personal interests and activities. Your answers to these sections in particular will be used as the basis of further questions at an interview, and your ability to put down a few coherent thoughts may decide whether or not you get to that stage.

Here are some notes to bear in mind when filling in application forms:

- Read the instructions and follow them to the letter.

- Make a copy of the application form and draft your answers before making a start on the real thing.

- Be succinct – you will probably not have enough space to be verbose.

- Put in as much research as you would for any other application. Keep going back to the original advert and read especially carefully any extra information that may be supplied with the application form.

- Include your CV with your application form if you believe it will add to the information given.

- Check and double-check for spelling and grammatical errors. If you have made a howler on the form itself and you have time to obtain another form, do so rather than using liquid paper.

- A returned application form should always be accompanied with a shortened version of the covering letter: 'I have completed your application form with regard to the position of Line Manager advertised last week, and am returning it as instructed.'

- Return the form before the closing date.

See also **References and Testimonials**.

LEGAL LETTERS

Legal letters can be divided into two categories: letters from solicitors and letters to solicitors.

Solicitors' letters

Letters from solicitors are a special category in that they are prepared by experts according to the laws relating to a particular situation. They are most often used to threaten legal action when a dispute becomes intolerable.

Some people are fond of instigating the dispatch of legal letters, but they should be reserved for particularly serious situations that cannot be solved any other way. This is first because of the cost of paying a solicitor to prepare a letter, and second, because the instigator may be running the risk of crying wolf once too often.

It goes without saying that the case should be discussed in detail with a solicitor before legal letters are despatched.

Letters to solicitors

The kind of letters most people will need to write concerning solicitors are those requesting their services. In this case, the first principle is that, unless it is a routine task, you should always try to discuss legal matters face to face with the advisor. Therefore, your letter need only give the bare facts and request a meeting.

Lay the letter out as you would any business letter.

Dear Mrs Eagle

Divorce Action
You have been recommended to me as a solicitor who specializes in divorce. My husband and I have split up and I would like to engage you to handle the divorce for me.

We were married for five years before we separated eighteen months ago. Our split was by mutual agreement, and I have his promise of co-operation in the divorce. There are no children. It seems that the procedure should be fairly straightforward, and I am eager to make a start as soon as possible.

Please would you telephone me to arrange a meeting. I would prefer an early morning or late afternoon next week if convenient.

Yours sincerely

See also **Disputes** and **The Law on Letter Writing.**

LETTERS HOME

There is a long tradition of letter-writing by those who are travelling or perhaps living abroad. Such letters can convey a detailed picture of a country and culture, and the traveller's thoughts and daily life. This kind of letter-writing can become like story-telling, and letters that tell a good story are very enjoyable to read.

When travelling, many people keep diaries to help them remember their observations, interesting events and associated feelings. The diaries can then be used as material for letters home, which are normally much longer than other communications.

- Give clear descriptions of places: weather, smells, colours, architecture.
- Bring to mind the impressions of the place that people who have never been there may have. For example, when we think of India, perhaps we think of palaces, snake-charmers, elephants, poverty, elaborate temples, spicy food, brightly-coloured saris. How far have your preconceptions and those of others been borne out by what you have experienced?
- Describe differences in everyday life between the home culture and the culture you are experiencing.
- How does religious observance affect daily life?
- Are people poor or wealthy?
- Is the food very different? Do you enjoy eating it?
- How do you communicate with others who speak a foreign language?
- How are you restricted by the local government? What liberties do you have that you do not have at home?
- Try to avoid mentioning bad things that have happened, unless you can assure the correspondent that you are still

safe and well. Try not to give your correspondent cause for worry.

- To prevent your letter rambling on, try to limit your material to one or two stories, along with some general observations .
- If you have received a letter from the correspondent at home, read through it again to see if there is anything to comment on. Encourage the correspondent to write back by showing how much the news from home is appreciated.
- Letters of this type are usually very informal. Use a conversational style, as if you were at home relating your tales from abroad.

See p. 93 for details of how to use a poste restante system. See pp. 291-3 for advice on writing to a pen-friend abroad. See pp. 138-49 for more general information on writing to correspondents abroad.

LOVE LETTERS

In these days of unfettered interaction between boys and girls, men and women, the art of writing love letters may well be dying out. Teenagers are glued to the telephone, and adults have ample opportunity to say how they feel without any impropriety being attached. And yet a well-written and sincere love letter is still a thing of the utmost romantic importance, an opportunity to say all those things that tie up your tongue – hopes, dreams, fond memories, words of appreciation and flattery. You might even wish to propose marriage by mail.

Love letters should without doubt be handwritten, and on the very best quality paper you can afford. It is not appropriate for a man to use scented or delicately-coloured paper. A solid cream or white watermarked paper is good. Women have a much wider range of stationery to choose from, but avoid the truly soppy!

The basic rule is tell the truth. In affairs of the heart deluding yourself or your loved one will inevitably lead to heartbreak. Never write anything you do not mean.

Breaking off a relationship by letter

Many people believe that writing a 'Dear John' / 'Dear Jane' letter is a profoundly cowardly way of breaking off a relationship. They hold that a face-to-face conversation, however difficult, is the only honourable course of action.

However, letters have the advantage that they give the sender time to formulate his or her thoughts clearly and to consider how to put them in the least hurtful way. The Dear John letter ensures that reasons are communicated in an atmosphere of serious reflection, rather than a torment of rejection.

As with love letters, be truthful and sincere. If there are positive points, mention them. Don't dwell too much on negative aspects and try to avoid expressing hurtful sentiments.

MEMORANDA

Memoranda (or memos) are notes used for communications within a single company. They are not normally placed inside an envelope, but may be if the contents are private or confidential.

Memos need no inside address, but the name and department of the recipient should be given. In the same way, they need not be signed, but the sender's name and department should be added. Some companies also use memos for general information to be communicated to all staff, either pinned to a notice board or duplicated and delivered to each desk individually.

Because memos generally act as informal notes, they need not strictly be written in the style of formal letters, but the information should be laid out clearly and succinctly.

If you are writing a memo to be pinned on a notice board, make sure that you give it a subject title that will draw the attention of passing staff. Memos are useless unless somebody reads them. You may even concoct a headline similar to a newspaper headline to draw attention (See p. 166).

Memos can be used for a variety of other purposes:

- To record the points covered or agreed at a meeting
- To request that a person attends a meeting
- To list the tasks being delegated to the addressee
- To pass on any information.

Memos should always be filed for future reference.

MEMO

To: **ALL STAFF**   Sender: E. W Davies,
Date: 15th November 1994   Dept: Personnel
                                             Extn: 2456

CHRISTMAS PARTY CANCELLED

This year, there will be no office Christmas Party as in previous years.

Instead, staff and their partners are invited to join the directors at Fishbourne Court Hotel on the evening of 21st December for dinner and dancing. Further details will be circulated next week. Those wishing to attend please leave their names with me before 30th November.

NEIGHBOURS

A good way to welcome and sound out new neighbours is to drop them a short note. The usual way to get to know newcomers to the area is to invite them to your house. However, it is sometimes difficult to know exactly what to say to people you know very little about. Here are some ideas:

- Do you and they both have children? Invite theirs over to play with yours.
- Do you and they have an interest in common? Invite them to attend a meeting with you, or to join your club.
- Invite them over for a drink/for tea or coffee.
- Mention a local event where you might meet – perhaps a meeting of the Residents' Association or Neighbourhood Watch Scheme.

The basic rule is to be friendly and welcoming and to avoid appearing to gossip or pry.

> *Dear Mrs Shanley,*
> *Welcome to Acton Road. It really is nice to have someone living at number 26 after it has been empty for so long – and nice to see new faces.*
> *Our daughters have already met at school, so I was wondering whether you would like to drop in for a cup of coffee one day next week. I have two children pre-school, so the place is always in uproar, but it's usually at its quietest in the afternoons.*
> *It would be lovely to get to know you, but obviously if you're too busy or want to wait until you're a little more settled, you won't offend by refusing. Give me a call – 5438765.*
> *Kind regards,*

NEIGHBOURS

The writer of this letter is careful to sound informal and easy-going. She points out a mutual 'interest', their daughters, and volunteers a little information about herself.

> *Dear Mr & Mrs Jones,*
> *Welcome to Newcross Drive. I hope you are settling in well, and that the house is well and truly warmed.*
> *My wife and I have invited some of our neighbours for drinks at our house next Saturday evening at 7 p.m., and I was wondering whether you would like to join us. We thought it would be a good opportunity for you to meet some people, and we will also be discussing a few matters connected to the Resident's Association, which you might be interested to join.*
> *Of course, the Resident's Association is not everyone's cup of tea, so if you prefer not to come this time we won't be offended. Let me know – 987984.*
> *Kind regards,*

The writers of both of the above letters have been thoughtful enough to give their new neighbours an escape route – a couple of reasons to refuse. Not everybody finds meeting new people easy, especially if they also have to get used to other changes, and not all of us like to meet numbers of new people at one time.

The salutation should always be formal unless you are already on first name terms.

See also **Disputes** for times when neighbournood relations are less amicable.

NEWSPAPER ANNOUNCEMENTS

Almost all newspapers carry announcements of births, marriages and deaths, and many also give space to notices of all sorts of milestones: coming of age, christenings, memorial notices, examination successes, etc.

When planning an announcement, check copies of newspapers for the column you would like to use. You will be asked to pay a certain amount per line of column space, or if you wish your message or notice to be placed in a box, you will be charged at a higher rate.

The wording of each notice is usually very similar, so check the papers in question. Below are some guides.

Births

Birth notices usually give the following information:

- The family's surname.
- Date of the birth.
- Christian names of the mother and father (and sometimes the maiden name of the mother).
- Place of the birth.
- Sex of the baby (son or daughter) and names.
- Names of other children if appropriate.
- Thanks to midwife or hospital staff if appropriate.

Smith On 15th Nov. 1994 to Dorothy (née Jones) and Edward, a son, (Michael James), a brother for Sharon and Edward.
Brown On 24th Sept. 1994 to Nichola and David, a daughter (Charlotte Kate). Our thanks to the staff at All Saints Hospital.

Deaths

With announcements of deaths, we return to formality. Give the following information:

- Name of the deceased.
- Date of death.
- A word on the cause of death (tragically, suddenly, after a long illness, peacefully, etc.).
- Age of the deceased.
- Mention the closest of the family.
- Place, time and date of the funeral.
- Arrangements for flowers or donations and name and telephone number of the funeral service if necessary.

Everyman On 20th June 1993, suddenly, A____ J____, aged 93, beloved father of Alice and devoted grandfather of Charles and Raymond. Funeral, St Peter's Church, Foxwoods, Friday 24th June at noon. Family flowers only. Donations if desired to RSPCA. Details: Co-operative Funeral Services, Dean Road, Foxwoods.

Acknowledgments

After a death and funeral, relatives sometimes prefer to express thanks for sympathy and support through the Acknowledgments column. It is usual to head the entry with the name of the deceased:

Everyman Alice Smith and the family of A____ J____ Everyman would like to thank most sincerely relatives and friends for their kindness and support in their recent loss. Also the staff of the Cardiac Unit, Foxwoods General Hospital, for their care and attention. Adam is sadly missed.

In Memoriam

These notices are published on the anniversary of a person's death:

Everyman, A___ J___, on 20th June 1993. Gone but not forgotten.
F___, Rose Agnes, died 16th April 1969. In loving memory.
T___, Frank Henry, died 25th May 1950. Lovingly remembered by brother Luke. Treasured memories.

Congratulations notices

On a lighter note, a coming of age (18th or 21st birthday) and passing exams is a time for congratulations. Notices are often given in columns or as display notices (in boxes). They are very simple to word:

Tim Davies Congratulations on your 21st. With love from Mum, Dad and Gina.
Tim Davies Congratulations on your exam success – BSc Engineering at Smartown University. With love, Debbie.

Engagements and marriages

Notices of forthcoming marriages (engagements) and marriages are discussed on pp. 309-12.

POSTCARDS

Everyone is familiar with the picture postcards available for tourists and visitors to send back home, but postcards can be used for a variety of other short messages. Most galleries, museums and card shops now sell a wide range of beautiful picture postcards, and it is useful to keep a stock for impromptu invitations, birthday greetings or other short messages.

Plain postcards can be used for longer messages, and may be personalized with the sender's name and address, which is usually printed across the top edge. If your postcards are not personalized, it is not necessary to give your address, but the date is always handy. You may also forego the normal salutation if necessary.

The size of the writing area on a postcard gives you an excuse to use a telegraphic (but not too cryptic) writing style, and perhaps even jot down a witty single-sentence message.

PRESS RELEASES

The writing of press releases is normally the domain of a body's press office or PR and marketing team. However, people with little or no PR background may wish to inform the press of developments in order to elicit some publicity. This is normally done by way of a press release, which is essentially an information sheet giving the major points.

On receipt of a press release, a newspaper or other publication may either make up a short article incorporating the information given on the release, or detail a reporter to find out more.

Notices of births, marriages and deaths are normally written out and sent to a particular department for publication in full. These are covered on pp. 257-9.

It is the editor's job to select the news and articles to be published, and any one press release will be vying for attention among a stack of others. Many newspapers now employ a number of editors, each covering a different section of the publication: home news, foreign news, women's interest, eating out, motoring, etc.

For a press release to be successful, it must first reach the right person, and, second, it must grab that person's attention.

Reaching the right person

There are two ways of finding out to whom you should send your press release. First, simply call the publication(s) you have in mind, and ask at the switchboard. Second, consult one of the press directories found in the reference sections of most comprehensive local libraries. These normally list publications by category (national newspaper, regional newspaper, magazine, etc.) and give the names and contact numbers of those people responsible for certain subject areas. It is just as well, however, to check with the publication that the person listed still holds the post.

Those running press offices know how important it is to keep an up-to-date list of contacts for press releases, and to keep abreast of personnel changes at the relevant publications. A good press officer often has a personal relationship with journalists and editors who specialize in the relevant field.

Attention please

Getting an editor's attention is the real skill in the writing of press releases. Avoid using banner headlines, or writing full press articles – it is up to the editors and journalists themselves to do this. Simply find a suitable, short heading and put down the facts as clearly as possible.

The subject should appear to be new, interesting and relevant. It is usual for the first paragraph to encapsulate the story, and for subsequent paragraphs to elaborate.

The release should be typed on headed paper, with the words 'Press Release' printed large. Many companies who send out releases on a regular basis print press release sheets as part of their company stationery, and often use colour in a bid for attention. However, avoid jazzy printing, because this can simply obscure your message.

Giving information

The release should always contain the following items of information:

- Heading.
- Date of the event.
- Date for release (see below).
- Name and address of body sending the release.
- Indication that photographs are available if appropriate.
- Name and contact number for the person who can give more information if required.

Within the body of the release, follow these rules for clarity:

- If you want to abbreviate a name or phrase, use the phrase in full the first time it is mentioned, with the abbreviation in brackets. In subsequent mentions, use the abbreviation only. It is not necessary to do this for well-known abbreviations, such as BBC, RSPB, etc.
- Write out the names of people in full, and always give their positions.
- Write out the names of organizations in full, and give their purpose or activity, if not widely known.
- Give exact figures and give them in full. Never give approximations.
- Write no more than 500 words at the maximum. More detailed information can and should be given as enclosures. Write on one side of the paper only.
- Give wide margins and use double spacing.
- Stick to short, simple statements of fact. This is not the place to prove your literary prowess.
- Remember the recipient and present the information with his or her knowledge and interest in mind. The language used for a release to a regional newspaper will be different to that used for release to technical or special interest magazines. For general interest publications, avoid highly technical terms and jargon. For specialist publications speak the specialist's language.
- If you are using more than one sheet, type the word MORE at the end of the first and any subsequent sheets. Type the word ENDS at the end of the release. Number each sheet.

Timing

The senders of press releases should time their circulation as well as they can. It's no use sending out information about an event taking place two months in the future if the publication is a daily or weekly – it will only be lost under the mountain of more immediate information. But give enough time for journalists to make further enquiries and to plan their coverage of your story.

If the information is suitable for publication in the next issue, it is usual to write the words 'Immediate Release' at the top of the sheet. However, there are some circumstances where information must not be published until after a certain time – perhaps the release gives details of a speech before it has been delivered, or of official figures before they have been announced. In this case, the word 'Embargo' is used, along with a date and time for release.

PRESS RELEASE

**SINGERTOWN OPERATIC SOCIETY
CELEBRATES 25 YEARS**

10th–16th June 1994

Immediate release

Attention: Ms Alison Bennett
Editor
Singertown Weekly News
46 Railway Row
Singertown
ST1 6TY

Singertown Operatic Society is celebrating 25 years of amateur opera in the town with a week-long festival of light opera in concert and performance.

Other activities include an opera-production weekend workshop, run by professional producer Harold Smith, and activities for children.

The week will culminate in a gala performance of Gilbert & Sullivan's *The Mikado*, attended by the Mayor, Anthony Cauldwell, followed by celebration supper. Proceeds to the RSPCA.

Full schedule of activities attached

Further information from:
Belinda Singer
24 Frederick Mews
Singertown
(0076) 098765

26th May 1994
ENDS

A less formal approach to letting the press know about items of news, is to write a short letter. This is especially appropriate if you are only contacting one publication, or if that publication is local. The following letter gives an example.

Dear Ms Bennett
<u>Singertown Operatic Society's Membership Drive</u>
Singertown Operatic Society is looking for new members. The Society has been in existence for nearly 25 years, but numbers have been dwindling recently, especially in the male voices. We are also short of people in the 20–35 age group.

Our 25th Anniversary celebrations (due in June) are in the planning stages, and we are looking forward to some special activities for anyone who likes to sing, act or both. Rehearsals begin now, and so this is a good time to join, meet some new friends and have the satisfaction of helping to stage a full-scale operetta.

If you would like to run a short article, I would be very glad to supply answers to any questions you have.

Yours sincerely

Belinda Singer (Mrs)
Secretary

QUOTATIONS AND ESTIMATES

Most people will at some time or other need to call in people to undertake certain jobs. Familiar examples are plumbers, decorators, builders, and so on. An important part of the early negotiations is, of course, deciding how much the job is going to cost.

An estimate is a rough guideline as to how much a particular person wants to be paid to do a certain job. The total price is based on estimates of the amount of materials required and the amount of time the job will take.

An estimate differs from a quotation in that a quotation should be a firm statement of price. You will no doubt find that the actual cost rarely tallies with the estimate, and the tradesman almost always underestimates.

Negotiating any job may take months of letters flying backwards and forwards. In the first instance, you may wish to invite someone to submit an estimate:

Dear Mr Robbins

I would like to have a wall erected at the front of my house, and would be grateful if you would let me have an estimate for the work.

I would like to use red brick to match the house and the walls to either side, and want the wall to be about six metres long and to reach a height of one metre. It must have secure foundations.

Please let me know as soon as possible roughly how much you would charge for this work, and how long it might take.

Yours sincerely

QUOTATIONS AND ESTIMATES

This initial letter gives a reasonably clear idea of the type of construction required, and the builder should be able to give a figure off the top of his head.

The next stage is to request a written quotation. Because the figures are fixed at this stage (or should be if there is no contradicting small print), you may need to supply further information, and the builder will almost certainly want to take exact measurements.

The quotation normally includes the tasks to be done and the materials that will be required. The price mentioned in the quotation should not normally be different from the final price of the job, but some tradesmen have a practice of tagging on extra expenses.

Always read the small print carefully. A quotation may say that the prices are fixed, but the small print may say they are fixed for only a short period, or it may even contradict explicit terms of what you consider to be your agreement. If the work is particularly complicated or expensive, it may be worthwhile asking a solicitor to draw up a contract.

REDUNDANCY AND DISMISSAL

Unless an employee is being dismissed summarily for gross misconduct, be sure to break the news gently and to give valid reasons for the move.

Redundancy

Most employers regret that they need to abolish jobs. Such cuts in workforce are made either to reduce overheads or to focus the company's attention on different markets. In a lamentably large number of cases recently, redundancy has been necessitated by bankruptcy.

When writing letters on the subject of redundancy, remember that it is a job that is redundant and not a person. Try to express appreciation of the employee's work and regret at the circumstances. But don't get too sentimental.

PERSONAL & PRIVATE

(Date)

(Name and address)

Dear Karen

<u>Notice of Redundancy</u>
As you are aware, the company has seen some very difficult times in recent months. I understand from the accountants that after the end of this month we no longer have enough money to pay staff, and we will therefore be winding up the company. It is with regret, therefore, that I must give you one month's notice of redundancy.

It has been a pleasure to work with you over the past year. It has been especially good to have your support in the last few difficult months.

I will, of course, write you a good reference, should you need one, and if you need time to attend interviews please let me know.

Yours sincerely

Dismissal

Unless a dismissal is the result of very serious misconduct, try to take the same softly, softly approach as you would with a redundancy notice. Give your reason clearly and without any sign of wavering in your decision.

PERSONAL & PRIVATE

(Date)

(Name and address)

Dear Ms Woods

Termination of Probationary Period
As you know, your employment here was agreed on an initial three-month trial period, which comes to an end on 30th June.

We have, of course, been monitoring your progress, and we regret to find that you have not reached our extremely high standards. I am sorry to say therefore, that we will not be requiring your services after 30th June.
I must add that on a personal level, it has been a great pleasure to have worked with you. I wish you the best of luck for the future.

Yours sincerely

Here is a summary dismissal:

PERSONAL & PRIVATE

(Date)

(Name and address)

Dear Ms Woods

<u>Notice of Dismissal</u>
Over the past few months you have been warned repeatedly to improve your time-keeping. Yesterday's unauthorized two-hour lunch break was unwarranted and, to my knowledge, unprecedented.

Please consider this notice of dismissal from the employment of this company as of the last day of this month.

Yours sincerely

REFERENCES AND TESTIMONIALS

A reference is a letter or oral communication describing or confirming a person's character. References are normally written by a person who knows the subject well: a teacher, employer or personal friend. It is normally requested by a potential employer, and written in response to that request, with the particular job prospect in mind.

Naming referees

Some prospective employers ask the job candidate to give the names of two referees. The employer will then write to the referee, and ask for a reference, giving details of the job applied for, and perhaps asking for specific questions to be answered.

Alternatively, the employer may ask the candidate if a previous employer can be contacted. Some candidates may find this awkward – they may have left previous employment under a cloud, for instance, or they may not have told their present boss that they are looking for another job. The candidate must be prepared to give a good explanation as to why a certain person should not be contacted, and the interviewer should be expected to respect those wishes.

Many people give the names of two referees at the foot of a curriculum vitae. This means that a prospective employer is at liberty to contact your named referees without alerting you. It is always best to know when this is going to take place, so a better way is to say that names and addresses of referees are available on request. (See pp. 237 and 239 for examples.)

Who to choose as a referee?

The custom is to choose one referee who knows you well, and has some standing or authority within the community. That person may be a member of the clergy, a business person, member of parliament or local councillor, or a teacher/school principal. It is important that this person has known you for some time, so that they can speak from experience. The reference given would contain information about your character and personal behaviour.

The second referee should ideally be your previous employer, or a person who has direct experience of you and so is well placed to speak about your conduct and abilities at work.

The well-connected job applicant will choose somebody who is well-known in the industry or perhaps known to the prospective employer. The essence of choosing a referee is to find someone who can speak with authority and relevance to your needs.

Permission to cite a referee

Before sending out a job application bearing a person's name as referee, it is essential that you ask permission to do so, and the most polite way to do this is in writing.

> Dear Mrs Jones
>
> As you know, I will be leaving school this summer after completing my GCSEs. I am now looking for a job in engineering and will soon be making a number of enquiries and applications.
>
> As my class teacher, I would be grateful if you would agree to act as my referee should I need one. Please let me know if you would have time to do this.
>
> Yours sincerely

This request is couched in formal terms, and gives the teacher an idea of the kind of employer she will be likely to hear from. The following request is a little less formal, reflecting a closer relationship between the sender and a former boss.

> *Dear Richard,*
>
> *As I think I explained the other evening, I'm quietly looking around for another job. The job I'm in now is too restrictive, and I would like more responsibility in a larger company.*
>
> *Would you mind helping me out by agreeing to act as a referee should I find the right job? I know we have not worked together for a number of years, but we do meet frequently, and I think you will still have some useful things to say.*
>
> *Can you let me know?*
>
> > *Best regards,*

Taking up a reference

When a candidate gets to the interview stage it is usual for the interviewer to tell him or her that the references will be taken up. At this point, the candidate can tip off the referee in readiness for the arrival of the employing company's letter.

Many employers have a standard form which is sent out to referees with a job description. Other, mainly small, employers simply give a description of the job and the company and give guidelines for the referee. Here is a possible letter, to be sent to a referee along with a company brochure and a printed sheet giving the job description:

> Dear Mr Pugh
>
> <u>James Long</u>
> James Long has applied to us for the position of store manager. He has named you as a personal referee, and I would be glad if you would supply us with a reference.
>
> I am enclosing a job description and a company brochure for your information.
>
> I would be grateful if you would reply in the next few days so that we can make our final selection as soon as possible.
>
> Yours sincerely

The following letter asks for more specific points to be covered by the referee.

Dear Mr Pugh

James Long

James Long has applied to us for the position of store manager, and has named you as one of his referees. We have interviewed him and he is on our shortlist of candidates. Before making our final selection, we are taking up all references.

I would be most grateful if you would let us know your opinion of Mr Long. Please would you ensure you cover as many of the following points as possible:

- How well do you think the candidate deals with the general public?
- Do you think that the candidate has a relaxed or strict management style?
- Is the candidate to your knowledge trustworthy?
- How long have you known the candidate, and in what capacity?

I am enclosing information on the company, and on the position in question. I look forward to hearing from you.

Yours sincerely

Writing a reference

Only agree to writing a reference for someone if you know that you can say something good about him or her. It is better to turn someone down than to agree and then have to fabricate your comments (potentially illegal) or say something detrimental. While you are probably justified to let a prospective employer know that the subject stole from you, and therefore not liable to be prosecuted for libel (see pp. 151-2), it would be better to avoid putting yourself in this situation altogether.

If you wish to decline giving a reference, there are plenty of excuses you can use. Probably the best is that you do not know the subject well enough. If the subject has not asked your permission to give your name, he has only himself to blame when you write to the prospective employer refusing to give a reference.

The following letter is a refusal in response to a request for permission to name a person as a referee:

> Dear Andrew
>
> Thank you for your letter asking me to act as your referee. I am afraid to say that I must decline. We have not met for a number of years now, and I feel I do not know you well enough to be able to speak authoritatively on your behalf.
>
> I am sorry not to be able to help. Good luck with your job hunt.
>
> Yours sincerely

If you have agreed to write a reference, the prospective employer should contact you giving enough information for you to be able to say something relevant. Consider the following points:

- How well do you know the candidate?
- Do you have experience of the candidate's work or personal life?
- Is the candidate trustworthy?
- Is the candidate hard-working?
- Is the candidate enthusiastic? Dedicated? Sunny? Serious?
- How well does the candidate work with a team? Is the candidate a loner?
- Is the candidate ambitious? Loyal?

Read the job description if you have been sent one (if not, perhaps it might help to call the prospective employer for an oral description), and note the qualities that the employer mentions as being important. Does the candidate have them?

If you are writing in your capacity as a previous employer, use company stationery, otherwise use personal writing paper.

Dear Mrs Biggins

James Long
Thank you for your letter of 19th March, requesting a reference for James Long.

I have known James for about ten years, since he joined the Buckby Local History Society. We have both been on the committee for a number of years, and James has acted as the society's secretary and chairman.

James is a natural leader and organizer. He inspires enthusiasm even among the most lethargic of our members, and never lets any obstacle stand in his way. He listens to the opinions and desires of others and compromises when necessary.

He has shown himself to be loyal and trustworthy, both as a personal friend and as a valuable member of the society. It is a pleasure to work alongside him.

I believe he would be an effective addition to your team.

Yours sincerely

Always be careful when writing a reference not to rely too much on the superlative, or your words will be taken as effusive bluster.

The next example is written in response to a general request for information about a cleaner.

> *Dear Mrs Hayes,*
>
> *Thank you for your letter asking about Mrs Andrews.*
>
> *She cleaned for us for about ten years while we lived in the area, and we found her to be hardworking, honest and cheerful. She took pride in her work, and rarely missed a day. We were certainly sad to have to leave her behind when we moved to High Town.*
>
> *I would heartily recommend her to you.*
>
> *Yours sincerely,*

Testimonials

A testimonial is similar to a reference. The difference is that it is written in the form of an open letter. Rather than being addressed to a particular enquirer, it is passed to the subject for future use. Because testimonials are not written for specific occasions, the comments in them must be more general than for a reference.

- No inside address should be given.
- Use the words 'To whom it may concern' and give the subject's name as the title.
- There is no need for a salutation, but give an explanatory signatory.
- Explain your relationship to the subject. If you have been an employer, give the subject's job title.
- Describe in general terms the subject's character and attitude to work.

To whom it may concern

<u>Angela Cartwright</u>

Ms Cartwright worked for me for six months in 1993 as a researcher and personal assistant. During that time she dealt efficiently with my general correspondence, telephone calls and other paperwork. She also proved herself to be a resourceful and hardworking researcher, thriving particularly on knotty problems.

She is outgoing in disposition and works well on her own initiative. She is thoughtful and pays due attention to detail. She was more or less punctual and frequently worked late when we had a deadline to meet. I regret that I have moved to a new neighbourhood, and so we have now parted company.

I would recommend Ms Cartwright as an outstanding researcher and PA, and feel sure that she would be an asset to her future employers.

Adrian Bisset
<u>Journalist</u>

REMITTANCE ADVICE

A remittance advice is a note that details the amount of a payment enclosed. Many companies now use computerized accounts systems that print the remittance advice as a tear-off counterfoil to a cheque. However, smaller firms may send out their payments by hand, and should always enclose a remittance advice with the payment.

The advice slip should detail:

- Date of the advice.
- The words 'Remittance Advice'.
- Payee's name and address.
- Date of invoice.
- Number of invoice (both the company's own number and the payee's invoice number if applicable).
- Amount of invoice.

Remittance advice could be written on a compliments slip (see p. 17), or forms can be made up as standards (perhaps using A3 or smaller paper), and the details filled in at the time of sending.

Remittance advice slips do not need to be signed, but they should give the name and address of the company sending the payment.

If receiving a payment, always check immediately that the amount on the remittance advice tallies with that on the cheque. Anyone opening the mail should note any discrepancies on the remittance advice, and forward it to the correct person so that the appropriate action can be taken.

REPRIMANDS

Most managers have found the need, at some time in their working life, to reprimand a subordinate for poor conduct, and most company policy dictates that this is done by letter, a copy to be added to the subordinate's work record.

Managers must think very carefully before issuing a reprimand. First, a clumsy reprimand could cause unnecessary tensions between boss and employee. Second, a reprimand will appear as a stain on an employee's record. Third, if this is the case, the manager may find himself in trouble, if accusations prove to be unfounded or malicious.

The first step, therefore, is to investigate the matter thoroughly. Only when you are quite clear what has happened, then put pen to paper.

The words you use depend on the situation. An employee may have failed to do something he was asked to do; in which case you might ask that it be done immediately and for an explanation of why it was not done before. You may even use a memo for this purpose. Repeated absence, however, can be a very serious offence, and so you are at liberty to use stronger words and even threats.

Here is a memo to cover the first instance:

MEMO

PRIVATE
To: John Soames
From: David Andrews
Date: 26th May 1994
Subject: Letters of complaint

I have received a disturbing letter from one of our customers, claiming that she has received no response to her letter of complaint, sent three weeks ago. As you know it is our policy to respond immediately, and that the burden of this falls on you.

I would be glad if you would look out Mrs Jones's letter (3rd May 1994), reply, and copy me. If you have a backlog of outstanding letters I suggest we discuss ways of dealing with them more efficiently.

Although no harsh words have been used, this memo still acts as a reprimand. Displeasure shows itself in the clipped, brusque manner. However, the message is tempered by an offer to help solve a problem if there is one.

The following is a letter reprimanding a staff member for fighting on company premises.

PRIVATE AND PERSONAL

(Date)

(Name and address)

Mr Burnes

Reprimand
I must make it clear to you that I take a very dim view indeed of the disgraceful incident that took place in the car park yesterday afternoon.

Your scuffle with Jim Broom was witnessed by several customers and members of the public, and has no doubt damaged the reputation of this company. This will probably be exacerbated by the police investigation now under way.

This company does not tolerate such playground behaviour. Differences must be settled in an adult manner, without resorting to fisticuffs. If you have a personal conflict to resolve, I suggest you do it away from these premises.

If you are ever again involved in an incident of this kind, on company property and in company time, you will be dismissed.

Hugh Latimer
General Manager

The seriousness of the letter is highlighted by the missing salutation and complimentary close. The General Manager also speaks on behalf of the company (rather than as a single individual) to make his point of view more forceful.

Legalities

Contracts of employment are governed by a range of legislation. Many companies have a standard procedure for reprimands and discipline. Be careful to speak within the law when issuing reprimands of this type.

RESIGNATIONS

Most contracts of employment stipulate that you must give a certain period of notice before quitting a job, and that you give this notice in writing. This situation calls for a letter of resignation.

Resignations are laid out as a formal letter, and the addressee's formal title should be used, even if you are on first-name terms from day to day.

The way to word a resignation depends very much on the circumstances of your leaving. You may have worked for a company for a long time, and be sad to leave, or you may have come into conflict with colleagues and be desperate to get out.

Before starting to write, consider very carefully your reasons for leaving. There is no reason why you should stipulate a reason, but there are circumstances where you might like to get it out in the open.

It may be that you have been offered a better-paying job, but would prefer to stay where you are if your present company would offer you more money. In this case it is valid to say all this, cross your fingers and hope that your boss thinks enough of you to bow to pressure and offer you a rise.

Dear Mr White

Resignation
It is with regret that I am giving you the required one month's notice of my intention to leave the company's employment.

I have been very happy in this position, and have especially enjoyed working in your department. However, a growing family means that I have been forced to seek higher-paid employment.

I will let you know the date of my departure as soon as it is fixed.

Yours sincerely

If you are forced to leave because of conflict, think very carefully about using bitter words. Although you are leaving, it might be better not to burn your boats by giving vent to your hostility – you may one day come across the guilty party in another context, and this could spell disaster for you. You may also be committing libel, and this could get you into even greater trouble.

Instead, give general reasons for leaving, and allude as subtly as you can to the root of your problems.

Dear Mr White

Resignation
In the past few months I have found it increasingly difficult to do my job with any effectiveness. I have repeatedly asked for support in implementing the structural changes we discussed when I took on this position, but this has not been forthcoming.

My efforts to do what is, after all, what you are paying me to do, have been met by the more entrenched managers with nothing less than obstruction and bloody-mindedness.

In this situation I have no alternative but to inform you that I will be leaving the company's employment at the end of next month.

Yours sincerely

(Incidentally, if you really do feel aggrieved, you may have a case for the courts, so you should visit the Citizens' Advice Bureau as soon as you can.)

THANK-YOU LETTERS

Letters thanking people for gifts, kindness or hospitality are easy to write and gratifying to receive, especially if someone has put in a lot of work to find a suitable present, or to entertain visitors for the weekend.

Thank-you letters should always be written promptly. Do not leave it more than a week after the event. All thank-you letters should be handwritten on personal stationery. While it is appropriate to use notelets or decorated cards, postcards are perhaps a little too offhand.

Letters of thanks for wedding gifts are covered under **Weddings** p. 319.

Thanks for a gift

Many children will start their letter-writing careers thanking relatives for gifts, but they often baulk at the task because they are not sure what to say.

Build up the letter in sections, using the following ideas:

- Thanks for the item.
- Name the item.
- Say why it is particulary appropriate or desirable.
- Mention other gifts received on the occasion (but try to avoid making it seem as if this particular gift is the least acceptable – a fancy T-shirt will certainly pale in the face of a new hi-fi system).
- Write a short paragraph of 'news' if you think it is necessary to stop the letter seeming too perfunctory.
- Thanks once again for the gift to close the letter.

> *Dear Aunt Bernice and Uncle Trevor,*
> *Thank you for your birthday present. It was a real surprise to receive it, and particularly exciting since I already have three coloured-glass bottles, and would like to start a collec-*

> tion. This one is one of the most beautiful I've seen.
>   There really hasn't been much happening here since we saw
> you last, except that David joined the local swimming club.
> He's a very fast swimmer and I'm sure it won't be long before
> he wins a competition. I just have to get down and study for
> the exams. They always seem to arrive so quickly.
>   *Anyway thanks once again,*
>   *All my love,*

Perhaps the most difficult of thank-you letters are for gifts that
are not gladly received. Perhaps they are inappropriate or just
unwanted. The knack with this kind of letter is to avoid fibbing
while still expressing appreciation. A thesaurus or dictionary
of synonyms may well come in handy.

> *Dear Aunt Dotty,*
>   *Thank you for the birthday present. It's always exciting to
> receive your parcels, and I appreciate the time you must have
> spent knitting the socks for me. The distinctive colour certainly
> makes them eye-catching. I'll think about you every time I put
> them on.*
>   *I hope you're still getting out and about despite the awful
> weather. I hope the rain lets up for your holiday next month. If
> I don't speak to you before then, have a wonderful time, and
> thanks once again for thinking of me.*
>   *With love,*

The writer has chosen her words carefully ('distinctive' has
been used, where 'garish' might first have sprung to mind), but
she has been able to lay emphasis on the sender rather than the
gift itself. In this way she manages to express appreciation for
Aunt Dotty's thoughtfulness and hard work despite the fact
that the gift was not to the recipient's taste.

Thanks for hospitality

Thanks for hospitality can be written along similar lines to thanks for gifts:

- Say thank you.
- Say how good it was to see your host(s).
- Mention why you enjoyed the stay in particular.
- Pick out one aspect of the visit that you enjoyed in particular (a meal, outing, relaxing in general).
- Extend a return invitation of some sort. You may not be able to reciprocate the scope of the hospitality you have received, but it is good manners to at least offer an alternative.
- Close with your repeated thanks.

> *Dear Dennis and Pam,*
>
> *Thank you for your kind hospitality last weekend. It's always a pleasure to see you both, and I think you know that I really needed the opportunity to get away from the rat-race for a while. Business is still tough, but after such a lovely weekend away, I feel more able to cope.*
>
> *Please drop me a line to let me know how Philip's exams go, and if you're coming to town, give me a call – while I can't put you up until I move to the new flat, I would love to take you both to lunch.*
>
> *Thanks once again for putting up with me.*
>
> *All my love,*

Alternatively, you may be thanking a person for a party or meal. In the case of parties or other functions given by a couple, it is usually the hostess alone who issues the invitation (see pp. 220-1), and so it is the hostess to whom thanks are normally expressed.

- Thank the hostess and name the event.
- Say how much you enjoyed the event and point out a few reasons why it was particularly enjoyable.
- Mention a reciprocal invitation if appropriate and repeat your thanks.

Dear Jill,

Thank you so much for a wonderful dinner, James and I enjoyed the evening very much. We were especially glad of the opportunity to make complete pigs of ourselves with your delicious pancake desserts.

We are planning a housewarming party as soon as we get the new house into shape, and we would love it if you could come. I will let you know the details when the time comes.

Thanks once again for a memorable evening.

Kind regards,

Thanks for kindness

There are many other opportunities to write letters of thanks. A friend may have written a reference that helped in landing a job, for example, or may have put you in touch with a new business contact. If you are a student, you may have cause to thank a person who organized work-experience for you, or a teacher who worked with you after hours to get you through an exam. For all of these occasions, and many others, the formula is similar:

- Thank the person for their kindness/hard work.
- Say why their actions helped you or were important in the context.
- Repeat your thanks.

Here is an example, from a member of a society to a visiting speaker.

Dear Mr Cahill

Thank you for coming to speak to the Local History Society last Thursday evening. All the members thoroughly enjoyed your talk, and your photographs of the area before the Second World War were extremely interesting. Some of the members were particularly excited to recognize family homes and businesses in buildings that have since disappeared.

Your visit has stimulated the members to make a start on a new project to mount an exhibition of photographs of the area before the First World War, and we would be delighted if you are able to come to see our work. I will send you details in due course.

Thank you once again for taking time to visit us, it was a memorable evening for all.

Yours sincerely

See pp. 169-75 for more sample letters related to associations and societies.

The following example is to a referee who has produced a glowing reference for an acquaintance.

Dear Mrs Jones

Thank you for taking the time to write a reference for me. It must have been fairly complimentary, because Barkers' offered me the post yesterday. I hope I live up to expectations when it actually comes to doing the job.

The position is more senior than my current job at Stanmore Ltd, and the pay is so much better that before long, Susan and I should be able to put a deposit down on our first house.

Thanks once again for helping to make this all possible.

Kind regards

See pp. 272-9 for more information on references and testimonials.

TO A PEN PAL

A good way of introducing children to foreign cultures is to have them find a pen pal. Some correspondences started in childhood may endure for more than the first exchange of letters, to become long-standing friendships, even affording the opportunity for travel abroad and for receiving foreign visitors at home.

Some correspondences are started in order to provide practice at writing a foreign language, but many more are conducted in English. Apart from pen-friendships with people abroad, some people correspond with prisoners, in Britain, or with British or other prisoners in foreign jails. Some people also write to members of the armed forces serving overseas. The advice given here is geared specifically towards those with foreign pen pals, but others may find it useful when trying to find something to say to other categories of correspondent.

Cultural exchange

The joy in having a pen pal is to find out about that person's culture and way of life, and that goes both ways. So do not take for granted everyday activities or ways of doing things – your pen pal may find all these things fascinating. Think about keeping a diary to remind you of things that happen between letters, and keep up with the national and international news. Here are some topics that may bear fruit:

- Celebrations: what you do at Christmas, New Year, May Day, Easter, for birthday parties, weddings, christenings.
- Where you go for a holiday: what you do, where you stay, who you go with, what the weather is like.
- If you are still a student, how the education system works: explain levels of examinations, different types of school

and college, the qualifications you are taking.
- Explain the job you do, and how you would like your career to develop.
- Mention everyday events, and news about your family and friends.
- Give descriptions of sports, hobbies, musical activities – anything that gives a picture of your life.
- Talk about international news – events your pen pal may have heard of: your pal's national team winning the world cup, or taking part in the Olympics; international charities you may have contributed to.
- Mention colourful national events: Guy Fawkes night, Remembrance Sunday, a General Election, the Trooping of the Colour.
- Collect cuttings from newspapers to show your town, school, hobby group; take photographs of events.

Try to introduce subjects as part of the 'news': don't talk about Christmas celebrations in the middle of May, for example. Avoid writing a dry essay.

Style

As time goes on and you get to know your pen pal, your writing style will become much less formal. If your reader speaks English as a second language, keep your English simple (see **Writing Letters Abroad** for further information), and avoid English idioms (the hair of the dog, getting on like a house on fire, a dog's dinner), which may well be misconstrued.

The following is part of a letter to a pen pal in the Philippines, who speaks English as a second language.

> *Dear Cynthia,*
> *Thank you for your letter and the photographs. It is very interesting to see your family and try to work out which*

person goes with which name. Now I have the picture of your house, I have a much clearer idea of how you live.

Today was the last day of school before the Christmas holiday. We have three weeks off before we have to start back in January. Today we had a school carol service: the whole school met in the school hall and we sang Christmas hymns. Then we distributed our Christmas cards and gave our closest friends presents. Now I have to concentrate on buying presents for my family.

We will be celebrating Christmas on December 25th at home. My brother usually brings his wife and the two children, and we eat a large lunch including turkey, roast potatoes and herb stuffing ...

This letter is chatty without using difficult English idioms. It describes customs that are recognizable to a person from the Philippines (a Christian country), but mentions details that may be different.

TO AUTHORITIES

Letters to the authorities (local government, the police or courts, etc.) should be constructed as you would a business letter, and preferably typed.

In this case in particular, the person you are writing to is likely to be more sympathetic if you keep it short and give only the relevant information. A stream of abuse directed at your neighbour and her ferocious dog is unlikely to be very constructive. Think out first what you have to say. Marshall your evidence if you are including any, and consider whether this information might not better be supplied in an enclosure. Consider what action you are requesting (if any), and make that clear at the end of your letter.

One of the biggest problems in writing to the authorities is knowing who to write to in the first place. See **Information,** pp. 211-12 for advice on how to track the relevant person down.

TO A YOUNG CHILD

When writing to youngsters it is more important than ever to put yourself in your correspondent's shoes, and to try to imagine what it is that he or she would be interested to read, rather than sticking to subjects more suitable for adults. Keep your language simple (do not use words that a child might not be able to read or understand), and make sure that your handwriting is more than usually legible. Above all, avoid being patronizing – children can spot condescension a mile away, and a frequent response is to 'switch off'.

The following example is to an eight-year-old boy after a visit to his grandmother.

> *Dear Joe,*
> *How wonderful to see you with Mum and Dad last week-end. It was great fun to hear all your news, especially your holiday adventures. I remember that Grandad and I had a holiday in Cornwall a long time ago, and we really enjoyed ourselves, too.*
> *Mum tells me that you are taking some friends to see a film on your birthday. I wonder which one you will choose. Whichever it is I do hope you all enjoy yourselves and have a lovely day.*
> *Are you going to write me a letter? I'm sure you will have plenty to write about after your birthday, and it's always so exciting to get your pictures. I'm sure I will be able to find space on my kitchen wall for some more.*
> *With love,*

The use of the title 'Master' for a boy seems to have fallen into disuse recently, so the envelope for this letter would be addressed using his Christian and surnames in full. When the boy reaches about the age of 16, the title 'Mr' comes into use.

Many pressure groups exhort us in their handouts to write to our MP to declare our support of a cause or disapproval of action taken by Government. Some even go so far as to draft a letter for us to sign and send. Indeed, apart from casting a single vote at a general election, writing to our MP is one of the few ways we have to make our opinions known.

But writing to an MP can be useful in other situations. Some MPs champion the causes of individual constituents in cases of injustice and maltreatment by the establishment, so a letter to an MP may well be a plea for help as a last resort. Equally, if you agree with a particular position taken by your MP or the party, or, on the other hand, object violently to something your MP has said, let her know. This is one of the few ways to govern those who seek to govern us.

MPs can be written to at the House of Commons, or at the address of their party headquarters in the constituency. As a consequence of their position, MPs receive a large amount of mail each week, and much of this is dealt with by secretaries. For your letter to get through, you must put your position clearly and use strong arguments to persuade.

Exert your credentials

If you are qualified to speak as an expert on a particular subject, make that plain. MPs are rarely experts on every issue they seek to comment on, so your contribution should be particularly important to them.

Form of address

A member of parliament takes the initials MP after his or her name. If that person has no other title, he or she should be called Mr, Mrs or Ms/Miss, as usual: Ms Edith Field MP. If your correspondent is a member of the European Parliament, then the initials change to MEP, but the title remains the same.

See pp. 98-106 for further information on special forms of address.

TO ROYALTY

The relationship between royalty and subject is governed by the dictates of etiquette. See pp. 98-103 for the rules for addressing members of the Royal Family and other members of the aristocracy when writing letters. Here are some reminders:

- Most Royals have private secretaries who deal with their correspondence. Unless you are already in personal correspondence with a member of the Royal family, write to their private secretary in the first instance.
- Never refer to a Royal as you/he/she. Use 'Your Majesty/Your Royal Highness/His Royal Highness/etc'. See p. 98 for details.
- Royal invitations are considered to be commands rather than invitations. The wording of your reply should reflect this. See p. 222 for details.
- If writing to members of a foreign royal family, remember that you are not their subject. You will need to use a different form of complimentary close than you would were you writing to your own monarch. 'Obedient servant' is probably acceptable in place of 'loyal subject'.

TO THE BANK

Most letters to the bank are requests for information – how do I open an account? What services do you offer? In some cases it may be necessary to query an entry on a bank statement, or to request that an account is closed or transferred to another branch or into somebody else's name. Sometimes, people find themselves asking for overdraft facilities.

Letters to the bank should be treated as business letters. Most banks also request that you address all correspondence to The Manager, and it is best to observe that request.

Here are four letters to a bank. The first asks that accounts are closed and transferred into a new name combined with a request for information on a separate subject. The second asks that an account is transferred to another branch. The third is a query about an entry on a bank statement. The fourth suggests a way to request an overdraft facility.

Dear Sir,

Personal accounts 0234567 & 0456723
Michael Dean and I have just got married. We both hold personal accounts at your branch. We would like to close our separate accounts and at the same time open a joint account. Please would you let me know how best to do this, and send us any forms necessary.

In view of our changed status, we both also need to review our pensions. Do you have any information on pensions particularly suitable for young married couples? If so we would be very glad to receive it.

Yours faithfully,

Jeanette Dean (née Baker)

First, note how the separate subjects have been dealt with in two separate paragraphs to avoid any confusion. Second, the new wife who has taken her husband's name gives her maiden name in brackets. There is no rule saying that this should always be done, but the information is very useful in this context.

Dear Sir

Joint personal account 0963547
Following her retirement, my wife and I have decided to move to the village of Deepdene. We would therefore find it more convenient to use the Molton branch, and I would be grateful if you would transfer our account.

We are planning to move on 6th November, and will need the use of the new account as soon as possible after that date.

We have had an account at the Henton branch for more than twenty years, and I would like to thank you and your staff for your efficiency and courtesy during that time.

Yours faithfully

The writer's letter is short and to the point. It is important that he tells the manager *when* he would like his account to be transferred, and that he has written in good time. The last paragraph is a kind thought, which should go a long way in oiling the wheels of the transfer.

Dear Sir,

Personal account 0238018
I would like to query an entry on statement 81 (10th August 1994) for the above account.

This entry details a standing order to the value of £150 drawn on the account on 2nd August. I do not recognize the name of *the payee and do not recall requesting a standing order. Could it be a computer error?*

I am enclosing a photocopy of the statement with the entry circled. I trust that you will investigate this as soon as possible.

Yours faithfully,

Notice how the writer gives all the information necessary to investigate the matter quickly, and backs it up with a photocopy of the offending statement. She is also tactful enough to lay blame with a computer rather than at the door of any particular member of staff. She comes across as calm and diplomatic, and is far more likely to elicit a helpful response than if she had sent a letter full of insults and accusations.

The following letter is a request for a small overdraft facility.

Dear Sir

Personal account 0238023
I have recently finished my course at Henton College, and have been accepted as a junior technician at H.D. Baker and Sons. My salary has been set at £12,000, with a rise of 5% after the probationary period of three months. After that I can expect annual increases, and there is a good chance of promotion after two years.

I am due to start work on 3rd July 1995, but will not be paid the first month's salary until 25th July. I will therefore need an overdraft facility to carry me through the intervening month or so, and would be grateful if you would set a limit of £250. I would hope to pay off the debt within three months.

Please let me know whether this will be possible.

Yours faithfully

TO THE BANK

The art to writing this kind of letter is to explain fully your financial situation. Tell the bank manager why you want the money, and explain where you expect the funds to come from that will allow you to pay it back. Suggest a specific amount (pick a figure that is within your ability to pay back in a reasonable time), and give a period for the overdraft. Also, try to sound positive about your financial situation. Mention work successes – a new job, a pay rise, a promotion – to keep your bank manager up to date with your earning capacity.

Show the bank manager that, while you are experiencing a hiccup in your 'cashflow', you are still in control of your finances. If you manage to do this, your request is likely to be granted.

TO THE PRESS

Newspapers have long been used as a forum for public debate. Correspondents comment on the activities, policies and speeches of politicians or well-known public figures, or add their opinion to debates brought about by articles printed. Magazines also print interesting correspondence, and some pay small amounts for the privilege.

To stand a chance of being printed in a newspaper, your letter must first of all cover a subject related to the news or a current debate. You may wish to agree or disagree with what a previous correspondent has said, to comment on the newspaper's treatment of a particular story, or correct errors of fact. Equally, you are more likely to be published if your written style is clear and perhaps witty, or demonstrates a strong emotion: outrage, hilarity, anger, wholehearted approval.

- Mention the story/letter/article to which your letter refers.
- State your case.
- Give your credentials if they will establish you as an expert or interested party.

Expect your letter to be cut by editors whose job is to fit the words into exact columns of type. They usually do not remove items that are essential to the argument, but may occasionally do so through error. You are at liberty to complain if you feel a published letter has been rendered incomprehensible or changed materially by this process.

Letters for publication are usually addressed to the Editor, and should open with the extremely formal 'Sir'

Sir

Simon Jones's article 'Raising Racehorses' (1st July 1994) contains several major errors of fact which lead me to believe that he has not done his groundwork properly.

First, ...
Second, ...
Third, ...

Taking these three basic facts, it is clear that Mr Jones's argument falls at the first fence, and should never have left the paddock.

Yours faithfully

The publication will usually print details of who and where to write to (some even provide fax numbers), and a few minutes spent reading letters that have already been printed will give you an idea of the kind of letter you should write.

TO UTILITY COMPANIES

These days, most business with utility companies (electricity, telephone, gas, etc.) is done over the telephone, but there may be an occasion when you need to write, just for the record.

To make processing of your letter easier, always give the following information:

- Your full name (or the name of the person subscribing to the utility).
- The address for which the utility is registered.
- A customer account number if you have one.

As with so many letters, before you start jot down the purpose of your letter. Make a couple of notes and arrange the information in a logical order so that the reader can immediately understand what you are asking. Check the information you give so that there is no confusion.

In most cases a bill will tell you to whom letters should be addressed. In general, a sales department will deal with supplying a service, and a customer accounts department will deal with terminating a service or queries on bills. If in doubt, a short call to the company will elicit the information you need.

Letter requesting a service

Dear Sir,
I have just bought the house at the address below. There is currently no telephone line, and I would like to arrange to have one supplied.
I will need one line and facilities for two extensions. The property is residential.
I will be moving in on 16th December and it would be ideal if the work could be done on that day.
Please telephone me at the above number to let me know if

> *this will be possible.*
> *Yours faithfully,*

Note how in this case, the writer is between addresses. She gives the current address and telephone number at the top of the letter and the new address at the foot of the letter to avoid confusion.

Letter terminating a service

Dear Sir

<u>Customer Account Number 5609871 – Apt 2, 27 Rozelle Street,</u>
<u>Harmsworth</u>
Today I have just moved out of the apartment at this address, and handed over to a new tenant, Miss Mary Jones. As of today, she will be taking over all utilities including electricity in her name.

The last meter reading was 06273.

I would be grateful if you would sign off the account in my name and send me a closing statement at my new address at the top of the page.

Yours faithfully,

Here the problem of two addresses has been solved in a different way, by putting the old address in the title to the letter, alongside the customer account number.

TO YOUR CHILD'S SCHOOL

Parents frequently need to write letters to their children's teachers explaining absence or informing the school that the child will be absent. It may also be necessary to investigate incidents, such as accidents that have not been clearly explained.

Explaining absence

The only real reason a child should be absent from school is illness or some family disruption such as a bereavement. When the child returns, he or she should bring a letter to the class teacher giving an explanation. This simple mechanism alerts teachers to the possibility of truancy.

There is no need to go into elaborate details. Indeed, most parents do not have time to do so, and some also forgo the usual envelope.

> *Dear Mrs Jones,*
> *Tania was absent from school yesterday because she had a stomach upset. I believe that she is much better today, but I would be glad if you would keep an eye on her.*
> *Yours sincerely,*

Pre-warning of absence

No parent needs permission to take a child out of school for short periods of time, but it is courteous to let the school know in advance if this is what you will be doing. Examples are dentist or medical appointments or special events such as religious festivals or ceremonies.

> *Dear Mrs Smith,*
> *Tania has a dentist's appointment at 2.30 p.m. on Tuesday 25th May. Please excuse her from lessons at 2 p.m. I will meet*

> her at the main entrance to the school and return her to the
> building after the appointment.
> > *Yours sincerely,*

Investigating incidents

Sometimes things happen at school that may cause a parent to worry about the child's safety or education. It is always reasonable to want to find out the truth or to discuss educational matters with teachers or school principals.

> *Dear Mrs Smith,*
> *Yesterday afternoon, James came home with a black eye and a quite serious cut to his face. He says that he fell from a piece of playground equipment, but I would like to make sure that his injuries were not caused by another pupil. As you know, he has been the subject of bullying before, and I hope that this has not resumed.*
> *Please would you find out what the lunchtime supervisor has to say, so that I can rest easy that this was a simple accident.*
> > *Yours sincerely,*

WEDDING CORRESPONDENCE

Planning a wedding is probably the most complex task most people will need to accomplish in their private lives. On the correspondence front, it may involve some, if not all of the following:

- Newspapers announcements.
- Letter of congratulations on a person's engagement or marriage.
- Telegrams/notes of congratulations from those who could not be present at the wedding celebrations.
- Correspondence with caterers and suppliers of other services such as the minister, the florist and the dress hire company.
- Choosing or creating your own wedding stationery.
- Invitations.
- Replies to invitations.
- Letters requesting the services of friends as best man and chief bridesmaid.
- Circulation of the wedding list.
- Thank you letters to guests who sent gifts.
- Despatching of wedding cake to those who could not be present at the reception.
- Letters notifying guests of a cancelled or postponed wedding.

Announcing the engagement

It is normally the bride's mother who decides on whether to announce an engagement in the press. The choice is between the local papers and the national dailies (which will inevitably be more expensive, but have a certain kudos). One reason for chosing a national newspaper is to reach friends and relatives who are scattered across the country. This can be useful when the bride's family live in a different region to the groom's family, and the bride and groom together live somewhere completely different. Alternatively, opt to use a local paper and consult with the groom's family for the best publication in their district.

The announcement should be timed to coincide with any formal announcement to family and friends, and any engagement party.

A formal announcement of an engagement, such as those printed in the nationals, might run something like this:

Mr A B Blunt and Miss G H Rowe

The engagement is announced between Alan, younger son of Mr and Mrs C D Blunt, of Wickerswell, and Geraldine, daughter of Mr and Mrs W N Rowe, of Honeymede, Dorset.

It might also read as follows:

A marriage has been arranged (and will shortly take place) between Alan, the younger son of Mr and Mrs C D Blunt of Wickerswell, and Geraldine, daughter of Mr and Mrs W N Rowe, of Honeymede, Dorset.

Mentioning the parents

Complications arise when any of the parents of the bride or groom are divorced, separated, re-married or dead. In these cases you will need to substitute some of the wording.

If the parents are divorced but neither are remarried, the wife retains her husband's surname but uses her own initials, and a separate district of residence may be given: ' ... Mr W N Rowe of Honeymede, Dorset and Mrs H G Rowe of Greenvale, Cornwall.'

If the parents are divorced and the wife has remarried, the

wife takes the initials and surname of her new husband: ' ... Mr W N Rowe and Mrs J O Jaques of Honeymede, Dorset.' In this case also, a separate district of residence should be given if this is appropriate.

If one of the parents has died, the notice should include 'the late'. If the father has died, the notice would read: ' ... daughter of/son of the late Mr W N Rowe and Mrs Rowe of Honeymede, Dorset.' If the mother has died, the wording would go: 'daughter of/son of Mr W N Rowe and the late Mrs Rowe of ... '

In some cases, couples decide to do away with the traditional etiquette surrounding engagement and marriage. In this case, they would jointly announce their own engagement, perhaps using the following, very simple wording:

Blunt–Rowe
Alan Blunt and Geraldine Rowe would like to/are pleased to announce their engagement to be married.

Announcing a marriage

Marriages are often included in local newspapers in an article style, with a photograph of the happy couple. Information for this type of announcement is often quite detailed, and can be worded in a less formal and telegraphic manner than notices. You could include the following information:

- Full names of the bride and groom.
- Full names and places of residence of the bride and groom's parents.
- Date and place of the marriage and any reception.
- Details of attendants.
- The honeymoon destination and duration of stay.
- The place the couple intend to live.
- Remember to enclose a formal picture of the wedding for publication if space allows.

Price–Varley

Christopher Price, son of Claire and James Price of Cumberley Lane, was married to Fiona Varley, daughter of Janet and Antony Varley of Heath Drive, at All Saints Church, Cumberley on 25th September 1993. The bride was attended by her three sisters. After a reception at Cumberley Court Hotel, the couple left for a two-week honeymoon in Florida. They will make their home in Cumberley.

If either of the parents are dead or divorced/separated, follow the guidelines given above for alternative wording.

Writing this notice and sending it to the newspaper concerned should be done about two weeks in advance of the wedding (a professional wedding photographer can be asked to submit a photograph at a later date), so that it can be included shortly after the big event.

Congratulating the newly engaged or the newly married

It is acceptable for anyone who hears of an engagement or wedding to send a short note expressing their best wishes. See pp. 196-8 for some ideas.

Wedding invitations

Most couples opt for formal wedding invitations to be printed by a stationers or jobbing printers, who will be able to show you a wide variety of off-the-shelf designs.

The invitation should come from the people who will be hosting the event – usually the mother and father of the bride, but sometimes a friend, or even the couple themselves.

Whether you are having invitations printed in the usual manner, or are planning to use a less traditional format, you will need to include the following information:

- Name and formal title of the guest(s) – either handwritten at the top left-hand side of the printed invitation or in the space allotted in the body of the invitation.
- Name of the host(s).
- Name of the bride.
- Name of the groom.
- Venue for the wedding (Register Office or church – if it is a church, ensure that you give the address to avoid confusion with other churches dedicated to the same saint in the same neighbourhood).
- Date and time of the marriage ceremony.
- Details of any reception.
- Address for replies.

Here is an example:

Mr and Mrs W N Rowe
Request the pleasure of the company of
...............(name of guests)............
at the marriage of their daughter
Geraldine
to/with
Mr Alan Bernard Blunt
at St Andrew's Parish Church, Honeymede
on Saturday 11th May 1994
at 1.30 p.m.
and at a reception afterwards at
Honeymede House Hotel

14 Dewdrop Lane
Honeymede
Dorset   *RSVP*

It may be that you have decided to forgo the expense or cere-mony of a formal reception and would like to invite a small number of close family and friends to a restaurant or drinks at home. If you are planning to do it this way, issue formal invitations as above, but excluding the final two lines giving details of the reception. You may then like to send separate invitations (perhaps At Home cards, see pp. 220-21) to invite the few to the evening function.

When sending out invitations, it might be useful to include a map showing the location of the venue for both the ceremony and the reception, and a list of instructions for driving or arriving by train.

Remember to order the invitations at the same time as any other stationery (place cards, order of service, thank-you cards, etc.), so that they form a pleasing matching set. Remember also to read over very carefully proof copies supplied to you by the printer for your approval. Check the spellings of names, and all the details down to the last letter. This is your responsibility – if an error is found after you have approved the proofs, the printer will not normally reimburse you.

Informal wedding invitations

Some couples may wish to forgo the traditional formalities of so many weddings, and host the event themselves. This is particularly common in cases where one or both members of the couple are older, divorced, or have already set up home together. In these circumstances, you may wish to handwrite invitations perhaps on coloured postcard-sized cards or personalized stationery.

Remember to include all the relevant information – use the list on p. 313 as a check. Here is an example of a letter-invitation.

Dear Charles and Sara,
   We would be delighted if you would attend our marriage, at 10.30 a.m. at Oldhampton Register Office, High Street,

> *Oldhampton, on 24th May 1994. After the ceremony, we have*
> *arranged a buffet lunch at Gregory's Restaurant, Angel Court,*
> *Oldhampton.*
> *We do hope you will be able to come.*
> *Kind regards,*

Replying to a wedding invitation

Always reply to a wedding invitation promptly. The hosts will
need as much time as possible to organize catering, and it is
helpful to have numbers fixed at an early stage.

Follow the formulas given on p. 221 for replying to a formal
invitation (either accepting or declining). If the invitation is
informal, you may write a letter in return, without resorting to
the formality of the third person.

On some occasions it is necessary to decline an invitation
after you have already accepted. A bereavement in the family
is one circumstance where you might need to do this. Use the
same format as you did when you originally accepted the invitation.

> *Mr & Mrs J Bland regret to inform you that, because of a*
> *bereavement in the family/unforeseen circumstances, they will*
> *now be unable to attend your daughter's wedding at St*
> *Matthew's Church on 15th April 1994, or the reception after-*
> *wards.*

As with other formal replies, this needs no signature.

If you have already accepted an invitation and now have to
bow out, it is even more important to let your host know as
soon as possible.

Circulating the wedding list

A list of wedding gifts should not be sent out with invitations,
however efficient this may seem, and no guest should be made
to feel that he or she must send a present. Instead, those wish-

ing to send a gift should write to the wedding hosts at the reply address asking if there is a list, or whether the bride is registered at a particular store.

The wedding list should be typed, and it is useful to divide the presents suggested into price bands, from inexpensive to relatively expensive. The list can be sent out (normally from the bride's mother) with a short covering letter:

> *Dear Jean,*
> *Thank you for asking about Alison's wedding list. Here it is.*
> *She is registered with Stepson's Department Store in Honeymede, so if you find something you would like to reserve for her, you can do it by telephone using a credit card (06543-6543, ask for Bride's Book). If you find time to visit the store, you will find the department on the second floor.*
> *I am so glad you can make it to the wedding, it will be lovely to see you again.*
> *Best regards,*

Best man and chief bridesmaid/matron of honour

The best man is the choice of the groom, while the bridesmaids are chosen by the bride. Remember in choosing that the majority of the organizing on the day falls to the best man (he will also need to be able to make an entertaining speech), while the chief bridesmaid will need to organize the bride's clothing and marshal the other bridesmaids.

These days, such arrangements are often made in person, but it is still nice to send a formal request by mail, to make the occasion that much more memorable.

Letters of this kind can be informal, and lend themselves very well to humour, especially between people who are undoubtedly good friends. Remember to ask well in advance of the day – the chief bridesmaid and the best man will be invaluable help when you are plunged into the wedding arrangements.

Dear Tony,

Lynn and I are getting married in March next year, and I would be delighted if you would do me the honour of standing up for me as my best man.

If you agree, remember I shall expect you to arrange the biggest hangover of my life, and still get me to the church on time. Do you think you can manage that?

Alternatively:

Dear Tony

If you swear on your life not to let out all the skeletons from my cupboard, you might be in with a chance at being my best man next March.

How's that for a promotion?

Writing to a prospective chief bridesmaid calls for a similarly intimate style:

Dear Mary,

As you know, John and I have decided to tie the knot. As my closest friend, I would be extremely happy if you would agree to act as my chief bridesmaid on the day.

I promise you won't have to wear peach-coloured satin if you don't want to, only please say yes.

With love,

Correspondence with suppliers

A wedding brings with it a torrent of suppliers: florists, caterers, venue managers, entertainers, the list can be endless.

It is wise to carry out correspondence with these people in the following stages:

- Write asking for an estimate, giving as much detailed information as possible. Remember to include your price range. Write to several suppliers, so that you can compare their estimated prices. Many people prefer to do this on the telephone, but a letter in return makes it easier for you to compare the services of competing firms.

- When you have decided on the final details, ask for a quotation (you may still wish to send this request to several suppliers in order to find the best price). When this is returned, the price will be fixed. However, look out for small print that indicates that prices could fluctuate, or change without notice. This is possible especially if you are making arrangements a long way in advance.
- When you have decided on your supplier, write a letter confirming your order. Even if you have done the first stages by telephone, the order must be confirmed in writing. Give the date of the quotation and the price details. Ask for confirmation that your order has been received. At this stage you will also need to give the time, day, date and venue as applicable.

All letters of this kind should be set out as business letters. Remember to keep copies of all your letters (preferably typed) for reference when it comes to paying the bills.

Further information on how to word an order, and how to deal with quotations and estimates are given on pp. 267-8. For further information on booking a venue, see pp. 178-81.

Telemessages and best wishes

If you are unable to attend a wedding, a telemessage or letter/card with your congratulations and best wishes would be welcome. These are often read to the company by the best man at the reception, and so are particularly memorable if you can say something witty. You might trawl a dictionary of quotations for apposite quotes. Alternatively stick to 'sorry we couldn't be there on your big day'/'hope you have a wonderful day'/'good luck'.

Distributing cake

It is common to send pieces of the wedding cake to friends and
relatives who could not be present at the reception. The
stationer who provides the wedding stationery will probably
be able to supply cardboard boxes for the cake, and you
should include a card. This should give the bride's maiden
name in the top left hand corner, crossed out with an arrow.
The couple's married name and address should be printed at
the top right-hand side. The wording should read: 'With compliments on the occasion of their wedding', and the date of the
wedding should be given on the bottom right hand side.

It is not usual to reply when you receive wedding cake in
this way.

Thanks for gifts

After the couple return from their honeymoon, they should be
turning their attention to the most immediate chore – writing
thank-you letters to all those who sent gifts. To make this
easier, it is possible to have thank-you cards printed at the
same time as the other wedding stationery, but if you want the
thanks to be a little more personal, buy some decorated postcards or notelets and handwrite your message. Follow the
guidelines on pp. 286-7 for thank-you letters.

COLLINS POCKET REFERENCE

Other titles in the Pocket Reference series:

Etiquette

A practical guide to what is and what is not
acceptable and expected in modern society

Speaking in Public

A guide to speaking with confidence,
whatever the occasion

Ready Reference

A fascinating source of information on measurements,
symbols, codes and abbreviations

Weddings

An invaluable guide to all wedding arrangements,
from the engagement to the honeymoon

Card Games

A guide to the rules and strategies of play
for a wide selection of card games

Women's Health

Accessible, quick-reference A-Z guide to the medical
conditions which affect women of all ages

Prescription Drugs

Clear, uncomplicated explanations of prescription
drugs and their actions

What Happened When ?

Thousands of dates and events in one handy volume

(All titles £4.99)